SLINGSBY AND SLINGSBY CASTLE

BY

ARTHUR ST CLAIR BROOKE, M.A.
FOR TWENTY YEARS RECTOR

METHUEN & CO.
36 ESSEX STREET W.C.
LONDON
1904

SLINGSBY AND SLINGSBY CASTLE

PREFACE

I AM greatly indebted to Lord and Lady Carlisle for most kindly allowing me to examine documents relating to Slingsby in the muniment room, Castle Howard; also to Mr Reavel, late clerk of Castle Howard, for making me a ground plan of Slingsby Castle; also to Lord Hawkesbury; the Rev. E. M. Cole, Vicar of Wetwang; the Rev. M. Morris, Rector of Nunburnholme; and the Rev. J. C. Cox, LL.D., for reading portions of my manuscript, and giving me valuable hints. To the last named I owe more than I can say, for it was he, while living as my neighbour in Barton-le-Street, who first spoke to me of the interest to be found in local history, and his invaluable help

has always been at my disposal.   I have
to acknowledge the permission of Canon
Greenwell and the Clarendon Press to
reproduce some illustrations from " British
Barrows"; also permission from Messrs
Walker & Cockerell to reproduce a photo-
graph of a picture of the Countess of Shrews-
bury in the National Portrait Gallery.   I
have to thank the following for kindly
providing me with photographs : Miss
Ashton, of Didsbury, Manchester ; Mr
Arthur Topham, of Boston Spa; Dr
Smeeton, of Hovingham ; and Mr H.
Crowther, Curator of the Leeds Museum.

Charles Darwin in one of his letters,
writing on the subject of botany, advises
a complete list to be made of some little
wood or field, adding : " It gives an uncommon interest in the work to have a
nice little definite field to work on, and
not the awful abyss and immensity of
British plants."   Slingsby is the little
field whose history I have had to work

on.   I cannot pretend to have made a
complete list of the interests of the place ;
but I trust the following pages will have
added some few things not unworthy of
commemoration to the story of Slingsby
and Slingsby Castle.

CONTENTS

CHAPTER I

SLINGSBY is one of a number of
villages situated along the southern
edge of the vale of Pickering, in the north-
riding of Yorkshire and the wapentake
of Ryedale. Pickering vale opens on the
east towards the sea, and is encircled in
other directions by three ranges of hills :
(1) The Tabular hills on the north ; (2)
the Hambleton hills on the west ; (3) the
Howardian hills on the south. The Tabular
hills have their name from their nearly table-
like summits. They extend from the coast
at Scarboro' westward to Black Hambleton (1309 feet), a tract of country which
Arthur Young speaks of as "not having
the epithet *black* given to it for nothing,
for it is a continual range of black moors."
At this point the high ground curves round

1

to the south, forming the lofty plateau of the Hambleton hills—a name somewhat fancifully derived by Eugene Aram in his projected lexicon from "*hemel*" and "*don*," signifying the " heavenly mountain " ; and given, he adds, to these hills, "not from their elevation, but from their figure to the eye, which is that of half a globe with the convexity upwards." The Howardian hills, the least elevated of the three ranges, extend from Gilling to Malton, and are called after the family of Howard, whose seat is in their neighbourhood. They seem to have been without a name until Marshall in his "Rural Economy of Yorkshire," written in 1796, so christened them (vol. i. p. 12).

A spur of the Hambleton range, called Cauklass Bank, runs into the western portion of the vale of Pickering, dividing it in this part into Ryedale, on the north, called after the river Rye ; and Mowbray vale on the south, called after the famous house of Mowbray. The vale of Mowbray, however, is not confined to this part of the vale of Pickering, but extends through the

gap, which at Gilling and Coxwold divides
the Hambleton from the Howardian hills
into the north-eastern portion of the vale
of York, as far north as the border of
Cleveland ; for the Mowbrays had possessions in all this region, their chief seat being
at Tresch (*i.e.* Thirsk), where they had a
castle.

Unlike the parishes of Barton-le-Street
on the east and Hovingham on the west,
both of which are of wide extent, and
include many townships in their areas, the
parish of Slingsby is small and compact,
and conterminous with its township, somewhat similar in shape to the human
shoulder blade. It measures about three
and a half miles from north to south, and
about a mile and a half at its broadest point
from east to west ; and has an area of 2570
acres. A supply of water being a necessity
of life, we find most villages grouped around
rivers or streams ; so Slingsby, like Hovingham, Gilling, Nunnington, and the rest,
has its stream or beck, Wath by name, so
called from the *Wath* or ford situated

on the old Roman road midway between Slingsby and Hovingham. A stone bridge, erected by the District Council in 1897, now marks the spot. Extensive views may be obtained from the high ground of the parish, and the airs that sweep over the sheep-walk, just within the gates of Castle Howard park, are an irresistible tonic to mind and body. In the spring, particularly when the east wind is blowing, the hills that encircle the vale of Pickering take a dark purple colouring delightful to behold. Geologically speaking, they belong to the Oolitic formation, a word that means "egg or roe-stone," and has its origin in the peculiar appearance presented by some of the limestones of this period, owing to their being made up of a number of small round grains, something like the roe of a fish, a structure that may be observed in almost any piece of limestone taken from the quarry at the head of the village, as well as in many of the stones of the castle. The term Oolite has, however, a larger meaning. It is not

confined to rocks having the appearance
referred to, but is given by geologists to the
whole series of fossiliferous beds lying between the Liassic and Cretaceous forma-
tions : nor are all these limestone rocks.
The Yorkshire Oolites consist, for instance,
of clays and sandstones, as well as limestones. They have been divided into three
main groups : (1) Upper ; (2) Middle ; (3)
Lower. The upper Oolites are represented
in our neighbourhood by the Kimeridge
Clay, which outcrops from under the alluvial
deposits of the vale of Pickering, in hills
or hillocks around Salton, Normanby and
Kirby-Misperton. The lower Oolites are
represented by the beds of the Estuarine
series, forming a tract of sandy ground by
Gay's Hall, and Hall, or Slingsby moor.
All the high land of the parish belongs to
the Middle Oolite, four beds of which are
represented : *i.e.* (1) Kellaways' Rock ; (2)
Oxford Clay ; (3) Lower Calcareous Grit ;
(4) Coralline Oolite. The Kellaways' Rock
(named from Kellaways' Bridge in Wilt-
shire) forms a belt of sandy ground which

rises and falls like the swell of the sea along
the foot of Slingsby Bank wood, where the
wood and the moor meet. Starting from
this point and climbing up through the
wood we soon come on a band of wet ground
stretching along the southern escarpment of
the bank. This is the Oxford Clay. Here
the Hard Fern (*blechnum boreale*) grows in
great abundance, but higher up the bank
it disappears, and its disappearance marks
the transition from the Oxford Clay to the
lower Calcareous Grit, a combination of
sandstones and limestones, which ranges
from Gilling by Hovingham Bank wood
and Slingsby Bank wood to Malton. If
we descend now towards the village we
come to the limestone quarry, where we
have the Coralline Oolite and Coral-Rag.

The Coral-Rag has its name from its profusion of coral life. It forms the upper-
most bed of the Coralline rocks. A fine
face of this rock may be seen in the
Slingsby quarry close to the roadway,
from which the branching stems of *theco-
smilia* and the spines of *cidaris flori-*

gemma have weathered out in relief. The Coral-Rag may also be examined at Nunnington station railway cutting, where it is overtopped by huge blocks of the Upper Calcareous Grit. This is a rare place for fossils, and the station-master is an enthusiastic collector.

Extending our walk we come to the village, built on sand and gravel, marked in the Geologic Survey map as glacial and post glacial. The limestone has disappeared. This is due to a fault or displacement of the strata. Some tremendous movement of the crust of the earth bent the Coralline Oolite down, or broke it off, causing a synclinal trough [1] where is now the vale of Pickering. Into this went down the Kimeridge Clay which lay on the top of the Coralline Oolite, and now underlies the superficial deposits that overspread the vale. The numerous wells in Slingsby may be accounted for by the depth and impervious nature of this underlying clay which

[1] See *Quarterly Journal Geological Society*, No. 231, p. 499.

holds up the water passing through the eminently porous and absorbent Coralline rocks. The clay has been removed from the Howardian hills by denudation, but on the north side of the vale it still remains in places, *in situ*, as at Appleton-le-Moor. The sand and gravel forming the subsoil of the village may be examined in the sand-pit in Greendyke Lane, where, the observer tired with watching the evolutions of the sand-martins, may turn his attention to the heaps of gravel, and extract therefrom quantities of *belemnites*, *gryphæa incurva*, and other fossils, all water-rolled, probably marking the shore-line of a great lake, which in the glacial epoch filled up what is now the vale of Pickering. Continuing our walk northward we cross the N.-E. Railway and come upon the low-lying land of the parish, consisting on the surface in part of fine clay (warp), and in part of sand with a little gravel ; originally, no doubt, extremely moist, and overgrown with low scrubby

trees, for this is implied in the word "Car,"
the local name for this region. Here
may be gathered the spotted orchis, tway-
blade listera, the bee-orchis, the moon-
wort fern, and other comparatively rare
plants. The place is also visited at times
by rare birds (see Ap. H.). The Oolites
are a peculiarly interesting formation in
some respects. In the literary history of
geology they hold an important place;
for it was while studying these rocks in
the Cotteswold hills around Bath, and
afterwards in the Hambleton hills, that
William Smith, a mineral surveyor, came
to the conclusion that all stratified rocks
might be arranged in a chronological
sequence, and could be traced over the
country by their relative position and
fossil contents. This discovery placed
English geology in the rank of a true
science, and has given to William Smith
the name of the father of English geology.
His geological map of the whole of Yorkshire published in 1821, a copy of which
is in the writer's possession, is a splendid

piece of work, and amazing to behold, when we consider that it was the production of one man working unassisted by previous observers, and amid all the difficulties which necessarily surround a pioneer of truth. Another thing which renders the Oolites interesting is the mode in which the Coralline Oolite has been produced. Corals have the power of secreting lime from the ocean; with this they form an internal skeleton; and when the colony dies, for they live in vast multitudes together, their skeletons remain; and in the process of the ages, a solid mass of limestone is formed. In comparison with the huge saurians that traversed the Oolitic seas, corals were but a feeble folk; but what they lacked in size was made up for by the immensity of their numbers, and the persistency of their labours; and as now in southern climes they may be found making "the dry land to appear in the midst of the waters," so once in the ages past they were at work where the vale of Pickering

now is, and round about it were coral
reefs washed by the warm waters of a tropi-
cal sea ; for corals cannot thrive below
a temperature of 68° Fahr.   Sometimes
when our winters are very severe, one is
tempted to look back with regret on the
warm and genial atmosphere of Coralline
Oolitic times, but this was long ago, in
the far away past of geologic periods ;
ages even before those times which we
call pre-historic, because although man
had appeared he has left no *written*
record of himself.

We have memorials of prehistoric time
in the tumuli on Hall Moor, lying to the
south of Slingsby Bank wood.   We give
an illustration of one of the largest.   It
imparts a touch of romance to the natural
beauty of this part of the parish to recognise
that the mounds that are scattered about
have a story to tell, that they are the burial
places of by-gone heroes, relics of an age
when all the complicated machinery of
modern civilisation was taking its rise in
the simple arts and crafts of primitive man.

Canon Greenwell examined about 200 tumuli in the north of England, and has given the results of his labours in " British Barrows." He opened thirteen in Slingsby parish, and writes with respect to them as follows : " All were burials after cremation, a practice which seems to have been the rule in this part of Yorkshire ; the number of incense-cups found with the interments is a remarkable feature, being very much beyond the ordinary proportion." In one barrow he found a broken cinerary urn filled with a deposit of burnt bones, amongst which were a barbed arrow point of flint calcined (fig. 1), a calcined bone pin (fig. 2), and a bone fibula (or dress-fastener) calcined, very neatly and ingeniously made from the articulating end of a small animal bone (fig. 3). The burning of the dead was probably a ceremonial rite, and it is thought that the vessels, to which the name of incense-cups is given, were used to convey the fire to light the pile. They are only found with burnt bones, are smaller than

other vessels, and nearly always have
holes drilled in them, which would serve
the purpose of supplying the necessary
air to the fire.   Incense cups vary
in shape.   The most common form is
seen in fig. 4, where the cup ex-
pands from the mouth towards the
middle, and then contracts towards the
base.   The ornamental lines on the
cup have been made by the impression
of twisted thong or cord on the moist
clay.   The usual practice of placing
mounds containing ancient interments on
high ground was broken through in the
case of Slingsby, for "the barrows,"
writes Greenwell, "with one exception,
were not on the lowest ground in the
valley, but on the slope of the hill-sides
which skirt it; in no case, however, were
they upon the ridge, or even high up the
side of the flanking hills" ("Brit. Bar.,"
p. 347).

The contents of the Slingsby barrows
were presented by Canon Greenwell to
the British Museum, where they may now

be seen in the first room at the head of the staircase on the left. There are five small elegant incense-cups, two large cinerary urns, and other smaller objects. The case containing them is thus labelled: "The greater prevalence of stone implements over bronze, and the fact that the latter are of the simplest forms show that the burials may be referred to the earliest bronze period."

All the barrows on Slingsby moor are round or circular-shaped, the long being exceedingly rare in Yorkshire. The long barrows are the work of an earlier race, living before the introduction of the use of metal; whereas the round barrows belong to the age when stone was giving place to bronze as a workable material. Various theories have been put forth to explain the custom of placing articles (weapons, implements, ornaments, etc., etc.) in these grave-mounds. It has been traced to ancestor worship, such as is common in China, in which case the articles referred to would be votive offerings to the dead. Some see in the practice a belief in immortality, and a desire on the part of the survivors to furnish the spirits of the dead with things supposed to be needful for them in the spirit land; others point to the superstitious fears with which the dead were looked upon, and suggest that the objects interred with them, were for the purpose of laying the ghost which was predicated by primitive races with an intense longing to return to earth and to the warmth and shelter of the hut wherein the living enjoyed themselves; but the living, it is thought, were not at all anxious to receive these ghostly visitations, and strove to provide against them by making the abodes of the dead as comfortable as possible, filling them with copious supplies of food, drink, trinkets, and everything that might be supposed to reconcile a spirit to its apartments underground. The custom, whatever be its explanation, is one to which the antiquary must be for ever grateful, for it has furnished him with materials for reading the history of the remote past. It has enabled him to divide prehistoric time into three periods : (1) the age of stone; (2) the bronze age; (3) the age of iron; and to further subdivide the first of these into two distinct stages in accordance with the degree of advancement in the working and polishing up of the material —*i.e.* the Palæolithic or old stone age; and the Neolithic or new stone age. These divisions are not intended to imply that the several ages can be separated off from one another by hard and fast lines; on the contrary, they gradually and imperceptibly merge one into the other. Thus, at the close of Neolithic times, we come across traces of bronze implements, which become more and more frequent until bronze becomes the paramount material; whilst at the end of the bronze age, iron gradually succeeds to and supersedes bronze. It is not to be imagined that all countries passed through these stages at the same time. There are countries now where the natives are in the stone age, as in the wild parts of Queensland, where, according to the report of modern travellers, the weapons and tools produced by the aborigines are all made of stone, shell, bone, or wood.   In like manner we find here and there in modern times, even in civilised countries, people who may be said to be intellectually prehistoric.   Thus Andrew Lang quotes the case of an Irish widow in Derry, who killed her deceased husband's horse, and when remonstrated with by the landlord, replied, "Would you have my man go afoot in the next world" ("Custom and Myth," p. 11).

With the help of the contents of the round barrows, we may build up something of the life of the folk who made them.   They were a short or "round-headed" people, as their skulls testify, and not as the builders of the long barrows, "long-headed."   They had advanced considerably beyond their "long-headed" predecessors; had passed the hunting-stage ; had flocks and herds ; knew something of agriculture ; made pottery ; understood the use of the bow and arrow ; and were clothed, as the buttons and pins prove. They had also some sense of art and refinement, and delighted to deck themselves with ornaments, such as beads, necklaces of amber, jet and glass.

It was my good fortune, in September 1893, to be present at the opening of a round barrow on the Marton estate, Flamboro'. It was with a strange feeling of awe and a certain fascination that we, a group of nineteenth century folk, stood upon the margin of the grave and looked down upon the principal burial—a skeleton of a large adult male lying on his side—some great hero, perchance, who in life had earned a name, and was carried to his last resting-place, it may have been, with the sacrifice of young slaves, for the mound contained the calcined bones of four children.

With respect to the age of the round barrows, "there is greater probability,"

writes Canon Greenwell, "of post-dating
than of ante-dating them ; but we need
not fear that we are attributing too high
an antiquity to them if we say that they
belong to a period which centres more or
less in B.C. 500" ("Brit. Barrows," p. 131).
To a somewhat later period may be
assigned the remarkable entrenchment
that may be traced running along the
top of the Howardian hills, not far from
Wath on the west, to East-thorpe farm
on the east. These works may be best
studied on the Yorkshire wolds, where
they may be seen traversing the country
with a network of lines. They are supposed to be later than the tumuli, for they
are found in many places on the wolds
cutting into the tumuli. Broadly speaking, they have been assigned to a period
post-tumuli and pre-Roman, and we cannot be far wrong in claiming for our
Slingsby entrenchment a similar antiquity.
It consists of a single dike, or ditch,
running east and west, just a little below
the brow of the hill upon the south or

steeper side. It was most probably a defensive work, erected by the builders as a protection for them and their cattle against some foe, or, it may be, some freebooting tribe. It may have served also for some of the various uses that have been attributed to the wold entrenchments, such as a line of communication between one settlement and another, a passage for driving cattle along, a connecting link between water-supplies, etc.

As our barrows witness to a pre-historic people, who once inhabited these parts, so in the Celtic names which cling to some of the streams in our neighbourhood, we have traces of the tribes which succeeded these earlier inhabitants; thus, the Dove, a tributary of the Rye, and the Rye which flows into the Derwent, as well as the Derwent itself, are all names of Celtic origin. After repeated changes of population, we have in these names evidence that a people speaking the Celtic tongue once dwelt in these parts and wandered

about, observing the natural features of
the country; remarking that *here* the
waters of the stream flowed darkly (Dove
from dubh = dark); that *here* they flowed
rapidly (Rye from rhe = swift, cp. rein-
deer = running deer); and that *here* they
flowed in the plain, or clearly (Derwent
from dwrgwent = water in the plain, or
dwrgwyn = clear water). Again the
Celtic "cum," which signifies a valley,
still survives in the name Cum Hag
given to the wood that overlooks the
depression in which Ganthorpe Moor
lies.

This testimony of language is confirmed
by history, for we learn from Tacitus that
northern Britain at the dawn of the
Christian era was inhabited by a tribe or
confederation of tribes called the Brigantes.
They belonged to the Brythonic division
of the Celts, represented by the modern
Welsh or Cymri, and to be distinguished
from the Goidels, who came earlier, and
are represented by the modern Irish or
Gaels. Brigantia included the modern

Yorkshire within its borders. The Brigantes, partially subdued by Claudius, were completely subjugated by Agricola, Vespasian's famous general, at which time the north of Britain yielded as the south had already done to Roman military control ; then Iseur, the capital of the Brigantes, became the Roman Isurium, modern Aldborough. Ruined camps, altars, coins, tessellated pavements remain to this day to attest the existence of the Romans in and around our neighbourhood.

Shortly after my coming to Slingsby, I was walking home late at night from a distance, and, taking a wrong turning, I came to a place where two roads met, and being in doubt as to which to take, inquired at a cottage, and was told that the place was called "Cold Harbour." I did not then know what would have interested me and helped to beguile the tedium of the way, that this was believed until lately, when modern research has thrown doubt upon the theory, to be a common name for places where Roman villas once existed, which were for a time used as inns, but afterwards falling into decay afforded so inadequate and uncomfortable an accommodation for travellers as to earn for themselves this inhospitable title. It is, however, by the roads that they made, or " streets " as they were called, that the Romans are chiefly remembered. Some of these followed the lines of the ancient British trackways, but differed from them in being made after the great Roman style, broad and straight with " stabuli " or posting-stations at regular intervals, together with "mansiones " or barracks for the accommodation of the troops ; one such street must have run by Cawthorn Camp, near Pickering ; and the name " stape " given to a neighbouring hamlet is evidently a survival of the Roman " Stabulum." Another such street is known to have connected the camp at Malton with that at Isurium. It must have run along the line of the present Malton road as far as Hovingham, and from thence through Yearsley camp. (In Domesday, Everslage, a place of wild boars). The suffix "le street" attached to the names of the neighbouring villages of Barton and Appleton denotes their proximity to this Roman road, and Slingsby being in a direct line between these villages and Hovingham may be regarded as a "street village." Often must the serried ranks of the Roman legions have thundered along this way, and the Brigantes may have stood to gaze as the Roman official, who resided in his villa at Hovingham, swept by in his chariot.

In the year 407 A.D. the Roman legions were recalled from Britain in order to defend Italy from the Goths. The Britons, left to themselves, maintained their independence for a while, but were ultimately mastered by the Anglo-Saxons, who turned Romano-Britain into Angleland or England. They were pagans, and introduced the heathen worship of Woden, Thor, and other gods, and expelled the ancient British church.

"To Walys fled the Christianitie
Of older Briton dwelling in this ile."
CHAUCER, *Tale of Man of Lawe.*

But the English came not only to uproot,
they came also to build up, and as soon as
they had established their dominion, they
settled down in the land, introducing their
own language, laws, customs, etc. One
thing that they specially prized, even then,
as they do now, was the privilege of
having a home of their own, secluded, and
marked off from their neighbours : hence
the number of local names ending in
"ton" (from the A.S. verb "tynan" = to
hedge), of which our neighbourhood has
its full share : as, for instance, Barton,
meaning the bear or crop-enclosure, which
was the beginning of the place; Swinton,
the swine-enclosure; Appleton, the apple-
enclosure; Salton, the willow-enclosure;
Fryton (Frideton in Domesday), probably
Freyr's enclosure, a Norse god : to which
may be added Colton and Broughton,
names that speak for themselves. Other
Anglian settlements are to be traced in

the terminations " ham," " ley " and " ford."
Thus we have Hovingham (Houingham
in Domesday), a place of mounds (houes)
and low meadows (ings), or taking " ing "
as a patronymic, the home of the sons of
Offa. Helmsley (Emleslac in Domesday),
pasture among elms.   Hildenley which
some connect with Hilda of Whitby, but
which may be a descriptive title of
the place with its hills, wooded vales
(den) and open glades (ley).   Ample-
forth (Ambreford in Domesday), a place
with a spacious or easy ford, a thing
much sought after in the days before
bridges, when fords were the only means
of crossing rivers.   Slingsby did not
exist at the time that these Anglian
settlements were being made, for it is,
as we shall see, a Danish village—the
place was probably woodland or waste ;
the forest of Galtres, which occupied
nearly the whole of the Wapentake of
Bulmer, containing within its boundaries
100,000 acres of land, lay to the south,
a tract of country in some parts dark with

trees, in other parts open ground of
swamp or moor, where barons hunted
the tall game, and robbers lurked to
waylay unwary travellers. Sutton was
at the centre of the forest, and on its
borders stood Tollerton, where the guides
took *toll* for their services. At Youl-
ton (Luckton in Domesday) a light
(lux) was hung out as a help to the be-
lated, as in the lanthorn tower of St
Saviours' church, York. R. L. Stevenson,
addressing the Samoan chiefs in order to
induce them to make good roads, told
them of what the Romans had done in
Europe, and "how to this very day you
might go through parts of the country,
marsh and brushwood, and suddenly come
forth upon an ancient road, solid and
useful as when it was first made, and see
men and women bearing their burden
along that even way, and blessing the
hands that made it." With some such
feelings we may imagine the travellers
through Galtres emerging from the
danger and difficulties of this wild region

upon the Roman street that linked Malton to Isurium, enlivened with the cheerful hamlets that had sprung up all along its course.

In process of time the Christian religion found a home in these hamlets: for there are carved stones in or about the churches of nearly all the "street villages" which testify to the existence of pre-Norman Christianity: Slingsby being an exception in not having any such relics. It was mainly through the instrumentality of Oswald, King of Northumbria, that the conversion was brought about. He sent for missionaries from Iona to teach his people. His name is perpetuated in Oswaldkirk; and in Stonegrave church may be seen some crosses belonging to this period, adorned with Celtic knot-work and figures. They are probably sepulchral, once marking the burial places of early Christian chiefs or priests. No doubt the Lastingham settlement would also have something to say to the early spread of Christianity in these

parts ; and perhaps also the monastery
founded by Oswy, brother of Oswald,
at Streoneshalh : a spot that must ever be
held in reverent memory by Slingsby
people ; for on its site looking seaward,
arose afterwards Whitby Abbey, with
which our church was connected for
nearly four hundred years.

CHAPTER II

THE MAKING OF SLINGSBY AND SLINGSBY IN DOMESDAY

A NEW element was added to our national life when at the beginning of the ninth century,[1] England began to be invaded by sea-rovers from Scandinavia, who came riding across the German Ocean in their black, raven-bannered ships, which they were wont to call their sea-horses. They came from the Vik, or great bay between Norway and Sweden now called the Skagerrac, from the rock-bound fiords of Norway and the level coasts of Denmark; and derived their name of "Vikings," or "Creekers," either from the Vik, from which they chiefly

[1] Freeman divides the Danish invasion into three portions, 1st for sake of plunder 795-850, 2nd for sake of settlement 850-950, 3rd for political conquest 950-1100.

came, or from the viks, creeks, or bays in which they loved to anchor.

This invasion is generally spoken of as the Danish invasion, because the Danes were probably the dominant race. The more daring spirits came first, for rapine and murder ; but in their wake followed others flying from the political tyranny of their kings, or seeking a new home in a land whose soil and climate compared favourably with their own. The bay of the Humber afforded a commodious harbour for their ships, and sailing up the rivers they spread themselves over the country, and with the aid of the names on the map we can trace the ways they took, and where they settled : thus, place-names ending in "wick," if the places be by the sea, or by a stream, may safely be derived from the Norse Vik : so Butterwick by the sweep of the Rye, may be Buthar's wick.[1] Other words denoting Scandinavian occupation are "by" and "thorp." The latter word is Danish, and means an aggregation

[1] Taylor's "Names and their Histories," p. 378.

of men or houses,—a village. We meet with it in the following place-names in the neighbourhood : in Coneysthorpe (Coungestorp in Domesday), originally the village of some petty king or chief (König), or perhaps the village owned by some court official; in Wiganthorpe (Wichinestorp in Domesday), *i.e.* the village of the Wick or Vikmen—a Viking abode ; in Ganthorpe (Gamelthorpe in Domesday), *i.e.* the village of Gamel ; in East-thorpe with which may be compared Stearsby (Esteresby in Domesday), both named from their eastward position. The terminal " by " or " byr " is from Danish " bua," to dwell. It meant originally an abode or single farm, afterwards a village. It occurs in 100 places in the North Riding, and in addition to our own village, in the following : Amotherby (Aimundrebi in Domesday), *i.e.* Aimundi's, or Edmund's abode ; Brandsby, the village of Brand, a favourite Danish name, meaning a sword or prow of a ship, and so suitable for soldier or sailor ; Brawby (Bragebie in Domesday) the village of Brage, the Danish god of poetry, also a Danish surname.

Of course if we would discover accurately the name of the first settler in any place, the man who made the "thorpe" or "by," we must go back to the ancient rendering of the word.   In old documents Slingsby is written Eslingesbi, Selungesbi, Slengesbi, Slyngesbi, all longer than the name in its present form, for, as Horne Tooke observes, "letters like soldiers have a tendency to fall out on the march." Eslinc is a Danish proper name, so Slingsby means the abode of Eslinc, that being the name of the man who first established himself here and made the place.

After building himself a dwelling-house, and surrounding it with a garth, having outhouses for his retainers and cattle, he would proceed to take in more of the woodland and waste, and soon a village would grow up around; the land of which would be partly demesne ; *i.e.* land retained for his own particular use, and partly land held in common by the village community.

Hunting and hawking would be the favourite pastimes of the little community, and feasting and hospitality would be constant, for the Sagas show plainly that every event of any importance was marked in this way.

It is not, however, in village names alone that the Vikings have left their traces amongst us. Many of the natural features of the country round about retain their nomenclature. Thus, when we call our small stream a beck (Dan bœk, Icel. : bekkr) ; the brow of the sheep-walk hill overlooking the spring, where the cattle love to rest on a hot day, "Kelbro" (Dan kilde, a spring) ; our low-lying land Car (Icelandic : kjar) ; the ditch with its trickling water-course between Slingsby and South Holm, the syke (Icelandic : sik) ; the steep escarpment among the Hambleton hills that is so prominent a feature in the view to the north-west, with Hode hill facing it, Roulston Scar (from skera : to shear or cut asunder) ; we are in all these cases

using the Danish tongue. Again, when
we pass by South Holm on the way to
Ness, we visit spots that the Vikings
must have seen and named: for holm
is Danish for an islet, or land which at
times is, or has been liable to be, surrounded with water, which must have
often been the case with South Holm,
before the dykes were erected which
now guard the streams to the north from
flooding the country. Ness too is Norse,
and means a promontory of land (cp.
Naze, Fr. Nez., Yorkshire Nab) ; and the
village stands on such a piece of land,
made by the sweep of the Rye. Again
across the moor to the south of Slingsby,
we come upon Thortle-wood, written
earlier Thurkil-wood, Thurkil being a
common Danish name derived from Thor,
the god of thunder, appearing again in
Thirkleby ; *i.e.* Thurkil's village. Further
to the west we have Howthorpe (*i.e.* the
thorpe upon the houe or hill), and Airyholme. This last is an interesting word.
It is written Ergunholme in Domesday,

and is derived from Horgum, dat. pl. of
Horg,[1] old Norse for a sacrificial stone.
The word is seen in transition in Dodsworth's Notes where it is written Argholme. Airyholme is therefore the holme
near the sacrificial stones. Opposite the
place, to the north, is a knoll of green
grass, called Hollin Hill, on the side of
which are some huge flat stones, the upper-
most resting on a roller of old oak. They
have all the appearance of having once
formed a heathen altar, and the fine old
oaks which grow on the hillside help to
confirm the impression. As we stand upon
the spot we are reminded of the lines:

> Beneath the shade the Northmen came,
> Fix'd on each vale a Runic name,
> Rear'd high their altar's rugged stone,
> And gave their Gods the land they won.[2]

Again there are customs still in vogue
amongst us that may be traced to Viking
origin, as, for instance, the payment made
by a master when engaging a Martinmas
servant, called "feste penny" ("Doan fæste

[1] Taylor's "Names and their Histories," p. 390.
[2] Scott's "Rokeby," Canto iv. 1.

penge," earnest money), as well as that
rough and ready method of expressing
public reprobation of certain disgraceful
acts, such as breaches of the seventh
commandment, or the beating of wives
by their husbands, which is known as
"the riding of the stang."   There are
folks in Slingsby who *mind the time* when
the stang was ridden for so-and-so.   Now,
however, it is seldom resorted to.   The
word "Stang" is Norse, and means a pole
or bar.   When the stang is to be ridden
for anyone, a procession is formed.   The
pole or bar is placed in a waggon, which
is dragged round the village by a noisy
crowd of men and boys armed with pokers,
sticks, pans, and every utensil out of which
discordant notes can be evoked; on the
stang or bar is sometimes placed a figure
of the delinquent, whilst one of the noisy
crew with a loud voice recites doggerel
verses somewhat after this fashion :—

> "Hey-derry, Hey-derry, Hey-derry dan,
> It's neither for my cause, or your cause
> That I ride the stang, but it's for " . . .

Here the particulars of the indictment which are made as ludicrous as possible are declaimed. It is usual for the procession to be repeated on three consecutive evenings, ending on the third day at the house of the offender; and some say he used to be burnt in effigy, and a silver coin demanded from him by his tormentors before they would be satisfied. The Norse origin of this curious custom is confirmed by history, which relates that Eric, King of Norway, had to fly from the hatred of his people for inflicting this stigma on a celebrated Icelandic bard. Again, we may trace Viking influence in some of our modes of speech, for instance in the answer often given when you ask after a person's health. " I'm not better, but I'm better than I was." Here we have the word "better" used in a double sense, in its old Scandinavian sense of " well," and in the ordinary sense in which we now employ the word.

In the mingling together of Anglian and Danish place-names throughout our district we have set forth one of the distinguishing marks of the Danish invasion. The Danes did not extirpate the Angles ; but both being from the same root, in process of time they became one people, and dwelt together side by side as members, as they really were of one family ; thus Slingsby, a Danish settlement, is situated between Barton and Hovingham, both Anglian settlements ; and Amotherby, another Danish settlement, between the Anglian settlements of Appleton and Swinton ; and when we come to treat of Domesday time, we shall see that of the fifteen berewicks included within the manor of Hovingham, seven were of Danish and eight of Anglian foundation. Mutual benefit arose from this blending together of peoples. The Danes learnt from the Angles the Christian religion ; witness the number of Kirkbys ; on the other hand much of England's commercial prosperity had its rise with the coming of the Danes, who were by nature traders, and had enacted for the encouragement of commerce that a merchant who thrived, so that he fared thrice over the sea by his own means, should be given the rank of a noble.   Much also of England's passion for freedom may be traced to the same source, for the Vikings, bred among the mountains and the sea, lived ever within the hearing of those two voices which have been described as "liberty's chosen music"; hence when in the ninth century the usurper, Harold Fairhair, tampered with their rights, many of them emigrated to Iceland, preferring to dwell in that bleak and desolate region with freedom to develop themselves than to live at home in servitude.   This was part of a larger emigration which in the course of the sixty years from 870 to 930 resulted in the colonisation of Iceland by the Norwegian aristocracy, an event which, for philological reasons, deserves to be remembered, for these colonists brought with them the old Norse or Danish tongue, which soon rose to the dignity of a literary language, and has remained in

Iceland practically unchanged to this day ;
whilst it has, in the Scandinavian countries,
degenerated into two literary languages,
Swedish and Danish, and into an infinity
of country idioms and dialects.   Hence
when we come across local names in
England that have an affinity with modern
Icelandic, we know that we are in touch
with the old Viking days before the
present changes which have made modern
Danish and Swedish had as yet occurred.

About the same time that some of the
Vikings were settling in England, others,
sailing farther south, landed on the coasts
of France.   Charles the Simple, consulting
his own safety, yielded to these ad-
venturers in the year 911 A.D. the fertile
territory on both sides of the Seine, close
to the sea that they loved.   Here they
dwelt, calling the land after their own
name, Northman's land or Normandy.
Under a series of dukes beginning with
Rollo they quickly acquired the language,
religion and refinement of the French
people, without, however, losing their pro-

pensity for roving and military achieve-
ment. The vicinity of England induced
many Normans to cross the channel,
and many English nobles sought Normandy for educational purposes, and in
the battle of Hastings the Normans under
Duke William proved their superiority in
arms. The north of England held out for
a considerable time after the subjection of
the south, but at length the whole country
lay at the feet of the Conqueror, who
parcelled it out into manors distributed
amongst his followers. Like the centurion
in the Gospel, "under authority, having
soldiers under him," each lord of a manor
or manors was at once both master and
servant—a servant to the king, from
whom he held his lands and to whom he
was bound to render a certain number of
knights in time of war, called his fee ; and
a master, inasmuch as he himself had
dependents, who were obliged to render
him certain manorial services. In this
way the king was the real owner of all
the land, and in 1086, twenty years after

the battle of Hastings, he determined to
know the full extent of his possessions,
and to find out all that was due unto him
from the whole country.   Accordingly,
commissioners were appointed, whose
business it was to go through the land
examining the people on oath, and in-
quiring into the nature and extent of each
manor, with the number and condition of
its cultivators; what its value was then,
and what it had been in the time of the
Confessor.   This survey, commonly called
"Domesday Book," either because it was
the king's judgment that spared no man,
or better, the book of the king's judgment
as to what was due to him, extended,
roughly speaking, over the whole of
England south of the Tees and east of
the Severn, and has an importance for the
historian that cannot be over-valued.   We
give the passages in Domesday wherein
Slingsby is mentioned.

In the index, page 84 *b*, of the facsimile
we have : " In Selungesbi Earl Morton
holds fourteen carucates " ; again on page

16 *b* Slingsby is omitted from the text containing the names of the other manors under Earl Morton ; but in a note at the foot of the page we have Nunnington and Slingsby put together, the record for Slingsby being as follows :—

" In Selungesbi fourteen carucates of land to be taxed. Land to seven ploughs. Two Thanes held this for two manors. There is a priest there at present with eighteen villeins having ten ploughs, and twenty acres of meadow. It was valued at 70s., now 30s." Then again on page 60 *b* Slingsby is put down as one of the berewicks of Hovingham manor under the head of land of Hugh, son of Baldric. The passage runs as follows :—

" Manor. In Hovingham Orm had eight carucates of land to be taxed. There is land to four ploughs. Hugh, son of Baldric, has now there two ploughs and ten villeins having four ploughs. There is a church and a priest. Berewicks—these belong to the selfsame manor, Wad (Wath), Frideton (Fryton), Holtorp, Eschalchedene (Scackleton), Hauuade (Heworth), Coltune (Colton), Grimeston (Grimston), Neutone (Neuton), Nesse, Holme, Eslingesbi, Butruic (Butterwick), Aimundrebi (Amotherby), Brostone, Newhuse, to be taxed together in all thirty-two carucates. There is land to fifteen ploughs. Two of Hugh's vassals have now there two ploughs and a half. There are present there forty-three villeins having fourteen ploughs and thirty-two acres of meadow. The whole manor with the places belonging to it were in King Edward's time valued at £12, now 100s. —wood—the whole."

It will help to elucidate the above if we take the passage relating to Slingsby under Earl Morton and add to it a few explanatory words.

(1): "In Selungesbi fourteen carucates of land to be taxed. Land to seven ploughs." The carucate or ploughland was the land tilled by one caruca or eight-ox plough: a somewhat variable quantity dependent on the nature of the soil, and the agricultural system in use in the place. There were two chief systems of agricultural management—one called the two-field system, the other called the three-field system. In the case of the first the whole arable of the township was divided into two nearly equal parts, one of which was fallowed every year. In the case of the second, the arable was divided into nearly three equal parts—one for fallow, one for winter, and one for spring tillage. When Domesday gives the number of carucates as equal to the number of ploughs, this implies the existence of the two-field system ; but when the number of carucates is double the number of ploughs as in our case, the three-field system is indicated. In an anonymous work entitled "Fleta," described by Maine in his "Village Community" as the "*Vade mecum* of farmers in the reign of Edward II.," it is said, "If the land lay in three common fields the carucate contained 180 acres—60 for winter tillage, 60 for lent tillage, and 60 for fallow ; but if it lay in two fields then the carucate contained 160 acres—80 for

fallow, and 80 for winter and lent tillage."
This would make the fourteen geldable carucates of Slingsby equivalent to 2520 acres.

(2): "Two Thanes held this for two
manors." We learn from this that in
Edward Confessor's time Slingsby had
two manors held by two Saxon nobles.

(3): "There is a priest there at present."
There can be little doubt that this implies
a church, and that Slingsby like Hovingham had a church at the time of the
survey. The Domesday commissioners
were not instructed to notify the existence
of churches, and although in some cases
they did so, certainly the whole number of
churches mentioned in the survey falls far
short of the number which we know from
other sources to have existed at the time.

(4): "With eighteen villeins having ten
ploughs and twenty acres of meadow," the
normal manor was divided into the portion
reserved exclusively for the Lords' use,
called the demesne—the home-farm as we
should say, and the portion held in common
by the village community. The villeins

were the men of the vill or village, the
tenants of the manor, working three days on
the Lord's demesne, and three days on their
own holdings in the common land, which
lay in great open fields not divided off by
hedges and ditches as now, but separated
into narrow acre or half-acre strips by
stones or turf balks. Each strip was
about a furlong (*i.e.* furrow-long) in length,
this being found in practice to be the most
convenient length for the drive of the
plough, and two or four poles in breadth.
Each villein had about a bovate of land
(normally one-eighth of a carucate, as
much as one of the eight oxen (bos) of the
co-operative plough could till), which would
not be all in one place but made up of a
number of strips in different parts. The
canadas or allotments at the head of the
village give a fair miniature picture of how
the open fields must have looked in the
time of the survey. The villeins could
not be dispossessed so long as they paid
their rent (usually a definite share of the
produce of the land), nor could their rent

be raised : on the other hand they were as
much a part of the estate as the timber
upon it, and when the manor changed
hands, they went along with it. In addition to the common arable of a normal
manor, there was the common pasture
where all the tenants pastured their cattle ;
also the forest or woodland which belonged
to the lord, but where the tenants had
the right of collecting fallen branches for
fuel, and of feeding their swine on such
acorns and beech-mast as they could pick
up ; also meadow-land and waste or un-
cultivated wilderness ; none of these are
mentioned in the Slingsby record except
" meadow," of which there were twenty
acres. This being of great value for hay
in winter would belong to the lord or be
let out by him at an extra rent.

(5) : " It was valued at 70s. now 30s."
The English solidus or shilling was not
a coin, but a subdivision of account,
equivalent to twelve denarii or twelve
pence. The only coin in circulation at this
time was the silver penny ($22\frac{1}{2}$ grains in

weight); the fall in the geld or tax from
70s. in the Confessor's time to 30s. in
Domesday time was due in great measure
to the depopulation wrought in the north
by William in consequence of the rebellion ;
30s. seems a small tax to extract from a
whole manor, but we must remember that
the bullion value of silver in Domesday
time was about three times its present
value. Twelve lbs. troy of silver were
coined into twenty shillings, now into sixty-
six ; besides the purchasing power of money
then was fully twenty-five times as great
as now. So that 30s. of those days was
equivalent for buying and selling to about
£37, 10s. of our money.

The mention of wood in the Hovingham
record serves as a reminder that a great
portion of the country at this time was
woodland. Here the swineherds tended
their swine, fed on beech-mast, acorns,
and such like ; and in the deeper parts of
the forest roamed, in addition to abundance of deer, the wild-boar, the wolf, the
badger, animals which have now been all

exterminated, with the exception of the badger, of which many fine specimens may still be seen, so much so that it is a practice on the part of some of the villagers of Slingsby to visit the Slingsby Bank wood on a summer evening and watch these animals playing around their holes.

The fact that Slingsby is mentioned as a berewick of Hovingham manor may mean that a portion of the township formed an appendage of Hugh Fitz Baldric's manor of Hovingham, or it may signify that a portion was held by Hugh in sub-infeudation under Earl Morton.

In Kirkby's 'Inquest' (Ap. A.) the number of geldable carucates in Slingsby is put down as fifteen, and not fourteen, which looks as if Hugh may have held the odd carucate and counted it in as part of his Hovingham manor, or it may be that the odd carucate, even in Domesday time, as in the time of the inquest, belonged to the Church, and being tax-free was not reckoned by the Commissioners. As in the Confessor's time two Thanes held in Slingsby. So at the time of the survey Slingsby was connected with two great Norman lords—Robert, Earl of Morton ; and Hugh, son of Baldric. Of these two personages we must give some account.

Robert was the son of Herlwine de Conteville and Arletta, daughter of Fulbert the Tanner. Arletta in her youth had been courted by Robert, Count of Hiesmois, afterwards Duke of Normandy. The story is that, looking one day from a window in the fortress of Falaise, he had seen her standing barefoot in the stream that flowed in the valley beneath, washing linen and chatting to her companions, and that, smitten by her charms, he had made her the mother of William, called, from the stain of his birth, "the Bastard," which name he, by his prowess, changed to "the Conqueror." Was it in scorn of his defamers or for his mother's sake that William delighted to honour his half-brother Robert? He made him Count of Mortain (Engl.

Morton), a town not far from Falaise.
Robert greatly promoted the expedition
to England. He figures in two, if not
three, of the compartments of the Bayeux
tapestry. He is at the king's side
in the battle of Hastings, at the feast
after the landing, and the figure represented as directing a trench to be
dug at Hastings is probably intended
for him. After the Conquest William
made Robert Earl of Cornwall. According to Dugdale, he was the most richly
endowed of all the Conqueror's followers,
enjoying in Yorkshire alone 196 manors,
and in Cornwall 248. He had a brother,
Odo, whom William also favoured. He
was made bishop of Bayeux when he was
but twelve years of age. He also figures
in the tapestry. He is seen at the battle
of Hastings riding a white horse and
wearing over his white alb a coat-of-mail,
whilst he wields in his hands a club, with
which he rallies the troops to the combat.
After the Conquest William made Odo
Earl of Kent, but later on, owing to his

overweening pride and masterful spirit, arrested him and kept him in continual imprisonment. This preyed on the mind of Robert, who pleaded so earnestly for his brother's release that William, on his deathbed, was constrained to hearken to his solicitations, not, however, without warning as to the result to be expected.

" I wonder," said the king addressing Robert, "that your penetration has not discovered the character of the man for whom you supplicate me. Are you not making petition for a prelate who has long held religion in contempt, and who is the subtle promoter of fatal divisions— a man not to be trusted, ambitious, given to fleshly desires, and of enormous cruelty ? He will never be converted from his whoredoms and ruinous follies. I satisfied myself of this on several occasions, and therefore I imprisoned not the bishop, but the tyrannical earl. There is no doubt that if he is released he will disturb the whole country, and be the ruin of thousands. . . . Whether I will or not your petition shall be granted, but after my death there will immediately be a violent change in affairs." [1]

These words were literally fulfilled, for Odo became prime mover in the rebellion against Rufus, and carried Earl Morton along with him. Eventually both brothers were besieged in Rochester Castle, captured, and sentence of banishment pronounced against them, and they sailed away from Pevensey, from the very spot where, twenty-two years before, they had landed on the way to the apparent fulfilment of their most ambitious hopes. This was in 1088, and the date has a significance, which will appear in our next chapter. Odo died in Palermo, and Robert in 1090 in the Abbey of Grestrain, founded by his father, and which he himself had endowed with lands in England.

Unlike the Earl of Morton, who spent his whole time in the south, and never seems to have visited his Yorkshire estates, Hugh Fitz Baldric may be said

[1] Orderic, bk. vii. ch. 16,

to have preferred the north to the south.
He seems to have had a special pre-
dilection for Yorkshire. Nothing is
known of his father, Baldric; and of himself, before he crossed the Channel, we
have only this—that his name appears as
a witness to a charter drawn up by a
certain Gerold, conferring upon the nuns
of St Arnaud, Rouen, lands and tithes,
in return for ready money to enable certain knights, himself among the rest, to
join William's expedition at their own
expense. These soldiers, it is thought,
arrived too late for the conquest of the
south, but not too late to take part in the
subjection of the north. Hugh had the
royal manor of Casterton in Rutland, two
manors in Notts, twenty in Lincs., fourteen
near Coxwold, etc., and in York four
mansions and twenty-one small inns. He
was much trusted by the Conqueror, who
made him Sheriff of York immediately
after its capture from the Danes in 1069,
being the second Norman who held this
office. To this time we may assign the

story related by Simeon of Durham,
which connects Hugh with the founding
of Selby Abbey. One day, so it was said,
as he was sailing down the Ouse, attended
by a strong guard—as travelling was
dangerous owing to the desperation of
the despoiled English—he drew near to
Selby, and observed, on a low bank of
the river, a cross, and a monk prostrated
before it. Having bid his men row to shore,
he landed, and inquired of the stranger who,
and whence, he was. The monk replied
that his name was Benedict ; that he had
come from the Benedictine monastery of
Auxerre, in France ; that praying there,
in his cell, St Germain, his patron saint,
had appeared to him in vision, bidding
him take a finger from his lifeless body
and speed across the sea to a river-side
habitation called Selby, and there found
a monastery. Hugh was much impressed
with the story, left his own tent as a
temporary shelter for the sacred relic,
sending carpenters afterwards to build a
chapel, and eventually obtained from the

king for Benedict that portion of the royal manor on which he had settled. Monks soon congregated. Thus was founded, through the instrumentality of Hugh, the Abbey Church of Selby. Benedict was the first abbot. He ruled the monastery for twenty-seven years, but proving a tyrant, was compelled to resign ; when Hugh de Lacy succeeded, by whom the great church, still remaining, was commenced.

After the death of the Conqueror, we hear no more of Hugh Fitz Baldric. He probably joined Robert and Odo in the rebellion against William Rufus in favour of Duke Robert, and in this way lost all his lands ; at all events, very shortly after this, we find Slingsby in the hands of the Mowbrays. But we must reserve for another chapter the work of tracing our connection with this and the other famous families, that appear in the history of the place.

CHAPTER III

SOME LORDS OF SLINGSBY

EXCLUSIVE of the Wyvilles, to be treated of in a separate chapter, there are five great families that have had connection with Slingsby—the Mowbrays, Hastings', Cavendishes, Sheffields, and Howards.

THE MOWBRAYS

The coast of Normandy falls away from England as it trends westward, until it meets Brittany—here an arm of land is thrown out into the sea—part of which is called the Cotentin, from its chief town Coutances. This district was the cradle of two remarkable families, the Mowbrays taking their name from Montbrai; a town not far from Villedieu, possessing a hill, Montebrough, of some elevation, with a streamlet hard by, separating the Departments of La Manche and Calvados, and

the Aubignis or Albignis who came
from the Commune of Aubigny, situated
east of the town of Periers. These two
families, neighbours in Normandy, were
afterwards more closely connected when
Roger d'Albini married Amicia de Mow-
brai ; and their grandson took the name
of Mowbray. In order to see how this
happened, it is necessary to refer to the
two brothers of Amicia de Mowbray
—*i.e.* Geoffrey and Roger. Geoffrey
was an ecclesiastic, and became Bishop
of Coutances (1048), which see he held
forty-five years. He had the character-
istics of his race, throwing strength and
vigour into everything he undertook. His
predecessor had begun the building of
the cathedral, Geoffrey finished it (1056),
obtaining funds for the work during his
travels and adventurous exploits in Italy.
He fought at the Battle of Hastings, along
with Odo, Bishop of Bayeux, assisting
afterwards at the coronation of William I.,
with whom he was a prime favourite, and
receiving as his share of the spoils 280

manors.[1]   Pride of birth, and love of
riches unfitted him for his sacred office ; and
it is with a sigh that the devout Orderic
records " This Bishop was more distinguished for military than for clerical
ability ; better able to array armed
soldiers for battle than to teach cowled
clerks in the chants of the Church."   His
name appears as one of the witnesses to
the foundation-charter of St Mary's, York,
at which time, in 1088, he was Earl of
Northumberland.[1]   Now, as this is the
year in which the Earl of Morton must
have been deprived of Slingsby with the
rest of his manors (see last chapter), it
is natural to suppose that it was then that
Slingsby came for the first time into the
over-lordship of the Mowbrays, and that
Geoffrey, bishop of Coutances, succeeded
Earl Morton as tenant in chief.   Geoffrey
died February 2, 1093.

Of Roger, the other brother of Amicia,
little is known.   It is chiefly as the father
of Robert de Mowbray that his name

[1] Dug. "Bar.," vol. i. p. 56.

survives. Robert, at the beginning of the reign of Rufus, joined the malcontent barons; afterwards he became a loyal subject, and, having inherited all his uncle Geoffrey's manors in 1093 [1] received the earldom of Northumberland.[2] He was lord of Thirsk manor, to which were attached in addition to Slingsby, the manors of Newburgh, Byland, Hovingham, Gilling. As in the case of Geoffrey, Robert's tenure of office was of short duration, for his proud and turbulent spirit would not let him rest, and, heading a conspiracy of Norman barons, who found in the Red King less and less to satisfy them the longer he reigned, he was besieged in Bamborough Castle in 1095, whither he had fled with his young wife, Matilda de Laigle. This rock-built stronghold, proving too mighty to be taken, the earl was lured out of the gates by a stratagem, and having been taken prisoner, was, by the order of Rufus, brought before the walls of the castle, which still held out.

[1] Orderic, bk. iii. p. 18. [2] Dug. "Bar.," vol. i. p. 56.

Matilda was then summoned to the battle-
ments, and bid to choose whether she
would open the gates, or see her husband's eyes put out.   It was not in woman
to hesitate in such an emergency; the
gates of Bamborough were opened; and
Robert, Earl of Mowbray, passed into
hopeless captivity in Windsor Castle,
where, at the end of thirty-four years of
prison life, death put a period to his
sufferings.   Before we part with the man,
let us look at this picture of his person
and character drawn by the pen of Dugdale :—" He was a person of large stature,
strong, black, hairy, bold, and subtle ; of a
stern countenance, few words, and so
reserved that he was not often seen to
smile ; stout in arms, disdainful to his
enemies, and so haughty-minded that he
thought it beneath him to obey his supe-
riors."   On the imprisonment of Robert
de Mowbray his estates devolved to the
Crown, until Henry I. conferred them,
along with those of Baron Frontebœf or
Stuteville, on Nigel d'Albini, second son

of Roger and Amicia d'Albini, for distinguished services.

Nigel was twice married, first to Matilda de Laigle, who, under a dispensation from Pope Paschal II., was divorced from her imprisoned husband. When no children came, Nigel, who desired an heir, having obtained another papal dispensation, divorced Matilda, and married Gundreda, the daughter of Gerard de Gournai (1118). The result of this union was Roger, who, by his grandmother's side, was a Mowbray, and who, by special command of Henry I., took the name of Mowbray (Camden's " Brit." and Dugdale's " Bar."), which thus became attached to the younger branch of the Albini family, from the elder branch of which family came the Earls of Arundel.

Nigel is always spoken of as the founder of the second house of Mowbray; although it was his son Roger who is said to have been so named. Roger was quite a youth, and a ward of King Stephen when he was taken by the barons to the

Battle of the Standard (1138). The circumstance is commemorated in one of the
stained glass windows in the Guildhall,
York, and in an old ballad of one hundred
verses. " Could we take a survey," writes
William Grange in his "Vale of Mowbray,"
" of the possessions of Roger de Mowbray
on his coming of age, their vast extent
would surprise us, and the largest estates
of England in the present day appear
insignificant in comparison. The 280
manors of Robert de Mowbray formed
but a small part of his patrimony. In the
neighbourhood of Thirsk he was owner
of the Castle of Slingsby and Gilling;
whilst on the western side of the vale
that bears his name stood the Castle of
Kirby Malzeard; so that his possessions
extended from the eastern to the western
moorlands." Camden, writing in the
same strain, says, " The family of Mowbray was as powerful and wealthy as any,
and possessed of very large estates and the
Castles of Thresk, Slingsby, and Gilling." [1]

[1] Brit., vol. iii. p. 153.

Roger and his mother Gundreda were liberal donors to the Church. Gundreda supported a band of wandering monks at Hode, where her uncle Robert de Alnetto lived as a hermit; and at her instigation her son Roger gave these same monks in 1143 the site for a house at Old Byland, from whence they were induced to remove by the difficulty of distinguishing their own bells from those of the neighbouring monastery of Rievaulx. After many wanderings they founded, in 1177, under the auspices of Roger, the abbey whose ruins may now be seen near Coxwold. Here their bells might ring without let or hindrance from Rievaulx; for six miles, as the crow flies part the two places, six miles of country as varied as it is lovely, for the road up the wooded hill, beneath which Byland nestles, loses itself in an upland moor, lonely and dark, and when found again, winds through a spacious deer park amid wide reaches of golden meadow interspersed with groves of larch, where in spring the cowslips and prim-

roses grow in passionate profusion, and
where, at a sudden dip in the slope of the
hillside, the great grey pile of Rievaulx
comes into view, seeming to fill the whole
valley of the Rye with its stately presence.
It is a walk which none should fail to take
who visit these parts.   The age was a
wandering age, and Roger de Mowbray,
notwithstanding all his possessions in England, was not content to remain at home.
He went twice on crusade to the Holy
Land, first in 1148, when he is said to
have vanquished a stout and hardy pagan
in single combat; and again, in 1186, when
he was taken prisoner by Saladin in 1187,
but ransomed in the following year by the
Knights Templars, to which body he was
a most liberal benefactor.

According to Dugdale,[1] he returned to
England, and, wearying of war, spent the
last years of his life in the seclusion of
Byland, where he died in 1202, and was
buried at the south side of the chapter-
house near his mother; here the bones of

[1] " Bar.," vol. i. p. 123.

this famous warrior rested in peace until moved by Martin Stapylton, in July 1819, and deposited in Myton-on-Swale.[1] We must not leave Sir Roger without recording the legend that on the way home from the crusade he slew a dragon which was fighting with a lion in a valley called Sarranell, whereupon he so gained the love of the king of beasts that he followed him to England to his castle at Hode.[2] It is probable that this legend was invented in later years to account for the Mowbray Arms, *i.e.* gules, a lion rampant, argent, which are now preserved among the quarterings of the houses of Howard and Berkeley. As it was the custom of barons to visit their manors from time to time, and to consume the produce of the land due to them on the spot, we may conclude that Roger de Mowbray would visit his sub-tenants in Slingsby, but what the castle was like, if any such existed at this early time, we have no materials for judging.

[1] Grainge's " Battles of Yorkshire," p. 20.
[2] Dugdale's " Bar.," vol. i. p. 123.

Roger de Mowbray had issue by his wife, Alice de Gant, two sons. Nigel, the eldest, died in the life-time of his father (1191 *circa*), and the manor of Slingsby passed from Roger to his grandson William, one of the knights who compelled John to put his seal to the charter. William died in 1222, and was buried at Newburgh, leaving two sons, Nigel and Roger. The former died without issue, and Roger became his heir and died in 1266. His eldest son, another Roger, is referred to in Kirkby's 'Inquest' as tenant-in-chief in Slingsby in 1284 (see Ap. A). In 1295 the king granted him free warren in his manors of Thirsk and Hovingham. He died in 1297, and an Inquest taken on May 8th, 1300, showed that he had two sub-tenants in Slingsby. John de Nyvyle, holding sixteen carucates of land as one knight's fee worth £16 per ann., and Johanna Wake holding five carucates as the fifth part of a knight's fee worth £10 per ann. (*vide* Appendix I., Grainge's "Vale of Mowbray"). The same inquisi-

tion states that Roger de Mowbray was
possessed of no Church living, and this is
in harmony with the Whitby cartulary,
which records that before this date Slingsby church had been presented to the
Abbey of Whitby. This Roger de Mowbray left by his wife Rose, sister of Gilbert, Earl of Clare, John de Mowbray as
his heir. He was governor of the city
of York, and afterwards of the Castles of
Malton and Scarboro' (1317). It is supposed that it is his effigy of stone that lies
outside the museum, at Scarboro'. The
shield bears the Mowbray arms, and the
lion is recumbent at the feet of the figure.
This effigy, it is said, was once in the
parish church of St Nicholas. If it is
at all a likeness of the man, he must,
indeed, have been a splendid specimen of
a warrior knight, with those huge limbs
and massive chest. He married the only
daughter of William de Braose, Lord
of Gower; and by the will of his father-
in-law succeeded to the barony of Gower,
but he was deprived of it by Edward II.,

who conferred it on his favourite, Hugh
Spenser.   This helped to kindle the
smouldering wrath of the barons, and they
marched to London and compelled the
king to banish the favourite.   In the
following year, 1322, Edward took ample
revenge on the rebels, and completely
routed them at the Battle of Borobridge,
when John de Mowbray with many others
was taken prisoner and put to death;
all his estates being seized into the king's
hands, and his wife and son imprisoned in
the tower.   Here tradition steps in to
adorn the tale, for it says that John de
Mowbray fled after the battle, and being
overtaken in a lane or "loan" between
the towns of Thirsk and Upsall, was
beheaded on the stump of a tree, and his
armour torn from his body hung up in
mockery on a neighbouring oak.   The
place still bears the name of "chop-head‧
loaning," and tradition adds that although
both oak and armour have disappeared,
the fearful peasant may still hear at midnight the clash of the harness of the ill-

starred knight upon the unseen branches, when the east wind comes soughing up the road from the heights of Black Hambleton.

Four years after the death of John de Mowbray his son, another John, was released from the tower, and restored to his father's rights by Edward III. He died of the plague at York, 1360. His successors continued to be over-lords of Slingsby by right of their lordship of Thirsk, until 1462, when John de Mowbray (vi.) died. Sometime before this the sub-tenancy of Slingsby had passed from the Wyvilles to the family of Hastings.[1]

HASTINGS

The house of Hastings derives its name from the town, one of the Cinque-ports, and traces its descent from a certain Robert, portreeve of that port, and dispensator or steward to William the Conqueror, from whom descended in the tenth generation Sir Ralph de Hastings, who had free warren in Allerston in the

[1] See documents in following pages.

wapentake of Pickering in 1329; and in 1344 purchased two parts of the manor of Slingsby from William de Wyville.[1]   In the same year he had licence to crenolate in Slingsby as appears by the following patent.

PATENT, ROLL 18, EDWARD III

For Ralph de Hastings to crenolate his house and enclose his woods.

The King, to all whom it may concern, greeting.   Know that of our favour we concede and give licence for us and our heirs to our beloved and faithful Ralph de Hastings that he fortify with a wall of stone and lime and crenolate his house of Slingsby, in the County of York, and that he hold this house so fortified and crenolated for himself and his heirs in perpetuity, and we concede to the same Ralph license to enclose a certain place called the Orchard of Slingsby, in Slingsby, and the woods of Slingsby, Firth, Colton, and Surkilwood, with the land there, in the said County, and that he hold the parks thus made and the place and the woods so enclosed for himself and his heirs in perpetuity, without let or hindrance of us or our heirs or the forest rangers, or any other functionary of the forest, so long as the place and the woods do not exist within the bound-

[1] Dodsworth's MSS. 1 fol. 21, b.   17 Ed. iii. "Agreement between Ralph de Hastings and William, son of William de Wyville, sheweth that the said William de Wyville conceded to the said Ralph two parts of the manor of Slingsby."

aries of our forest. In testimony of which, etc., this Roll at Westminster on the 28th day of January.

Private Seal.

Ralph Hastings could have had little time to carry out the provisions of the above patent, or to enjoy any improvements that he may have made in Slingsby; for in the year 1346, at the battle of Nevilles Cross he received the wounds of which he shortly afterwards died. He was buried at Sulby Abbey by his wife Margaret, daughter of Sir William de Herle, Chief Justice of the Court of Common Pleas; he became the father of an only son and heir, another Sir Ralph, whose Inquest post-mortem taken in 1401 runs as follows :—

INQUISITION POST MORTEM
3 HENRY IV., No. 64.

"Inquisition taken at Slengesby on Thursday, next before the Feast of the Nativity of S. John the Baptist in the second year of the reign of King Henry the Fourth (A.D. 1401). Before William de Skipwith, Escheator of the said Lord the King in the County of York, by virtue of his office, by the oath of John de Neuton de Calton, Thomas de Swynton, William de Colton, Richard de Clay, John

Wodecok, John Brian, Thomas de Holm, John Trop,
William de Mote, William de Semiŏ, John Hugsoñ,
and John Amyas, Jurors. Who say upon their oath
that Ralph de Hastyngs, Chivalier, de Slengesby,
died seized in his demesne as of fee of the Castle
and Manor of Slengesby, with (its) appurtenances
and members which extend themselves in Slengesby,
Colton and Houthorp and are held of Thomas[1] son
and heir of Thomas late Duke of Norfolk[2] as of his
Manor of Thresk by knights' service whereof (sic)
the said Castle and Manor of Slengesby are worth by
the year in all issues, saving reprises, £16, payable at
the Feasts of St. Martin in Winter, and Pentecost, by
equal portions. And they say that the Manor of Colton
is worth by the year in all issues, saving reprises,[3]
40s. payable at the same times. And they say that
the Manor of Houthorp with appurtenances is worth
by the year in all issues, saving reprises, £8 payable
at the same terms. And they say that the said
Ralph de Hastynges died on the vigil (of the feast)
of the Apostles Simon and Jude in the twenty first
year of the reign of King Richard the Second (A.D.
1397). And they say that Sir Ralph de Hastynges,
Knight, is the son and next heir of the said Ralph
de Hastynges deceased, and will be of the age of
twenty years on the feast of St. Bartholomew the
Apostle. In witness whereof the Jurors aforesaid
have set their seals to this Inquisition. Given the
day, place and year abovesaid."

---

[1] Beheaded 1405. [2] Banished 1368, died at Venice, 1400.
[3] Reprises were deductions and duties paid yearly out
of a Manor, as rent charges.

The above Sir Ralph had issue by his second wife, Maud, daughter of Sir Robert de Sutton, five sons; the third of whom, Sir Leonard Hastings, succeeded to the family estates on the death of his elder brothers, Ralph and Richard. He died on the 20th day of Oct. 1455; and about two months afterwards the following Inquest post-mortem was taken :—

ABSTRACT

"Inquisition taken at the Castle of York on the ninth of December, in the thirty fourth year of the reign of King Henry the Sixth [*i.e.* A.D. 1455], after the death of Sir Leonard Hastynges, Knight. The Jury say that the said Sir Leonard was seized in his demesne as of fee of, *inter alia*, the Manor of Slengesby with its appurtenances in the County of York, in which same Manor is a certain site upon which is built a castle which is worth nothing by the year beyond reprises. And of a certain close there called "le Orchard" which is worth by the year beyond reprises 6s. 8d. And of three several closes there of which each close is worth by the year beyond reprises six shillings and eight pence. And of ten shillings of the rent of assize there issuing annually from divers lands and tenements of divers free tenants there payable annually at the Feasts of S. Martin in Winter and Pentecost. And of sixteen virgates of demesne land with appurtenances there

of which each virgate is worth by the year beyond
reprises, five shillings.   And of twenty six virgates
of land there with appurtenances in the hands of
divers tenants at will, of which every virgate is worth
by the year beyond reprises, three shillings.   And of
sixteen messuages there of which every messuage is
worth by the year beyond reprises, two shillings.
And of four cottages there of which every cottage is
worth by the year beyond reprises, three shillings.
And of twelve acres of meadow there of which
every acre is worth by the year beyond reprises,
twelve pence.   And of a water mill there which is
worth by the year beyond reprises, ten shillings.
And of one wood called Thurkilwood there containing in itself fourteen acres, which is worth nothing
by the year but the waste thereof to be made (*absque
vasto inde faciend*).   And of a certain other wood
there called le Frethwode containing in itself twelve
acres which is worth nothing by the year beyond
enclosure (*ultra claus*) but the waste thereof to be
made.   And of a certain other wood there called
Erne (?) parke which contains in itself two acres
which is worth nothing by the year beyond enclosure
but the waste thereof to be made.   And the Jurors
aforesaid say that the aforesaid Manor with appurtenances is held of John Viscount Beaumont and
Katherine his wife Duchess of Norfolk[1] as in right

---

[1] Daughter of Ralph Neville, Earl of Westmoreland. She
married first John de Mowbray (v.), 2nd Duke of Norfolk,
and at his death Thomas Strangways, and afterwards
this John Viscount Beaumont, and lastly Sir J. Widville.

of the same Katherine as of their Lordship of Thrisk, but by what Service they are ignorant. Also the Jurors aforesaid say that the said Leonard Hastynges was seized in his demesne as of fee of one capital messuage with its appurtenances in Houthorp in the County aforesaid which is parcel of the Lordship of Slyngesby and is worth by the year beyond reprises, four shillings ; and there are there eight virgates of land, each virgate worth five shillings a year beyond reprises. And of one wood called Howthorparke containing fourteen acres, each acre worth nothing by the year beyond reprises, but the waste thereof to be made. And of ten acres of meadow there each acre worth twenty pence by the year beyond reprises. And of two acres of several pasture there each pasture (sic) worth five shillings a year beyond reprises. And of three messuages with appurtenance in Colton each messuage worth by the year beyond reprises, two shillings. And of seven virgates of land with appurtenances there, each virgate worth by year beyond reprises, five shillings. And of eleven acres of meadow there each acre worth by the year beyond reprises twelve pence. And of three cottages with appurtenances each cottage worth by the year beyond reprises, two shillings. And the Jurors say that the capital messuage of Howthorp and the lands in Colton are held of the said Lord Beaumont and his said wife, but by what service they are ignorant. The Jurors say that the said Leonard Hastynges died on the twentieth day of October in the thirty fourth year of the reign of King Henry the Sixth (A.D. 1455) and that William Hastynges, Esquire, is his son and next heir aged twenty four years and more."

The successor of Sir Leonard Hastings was the famous William Hastings, who in the year 1461 was created by Edward IV. Baron Hastings of Ashby de la Zouche, where he built a magnificent castle; in the next year according to the following charter (1462), he had licence to rebuild and fortify his houses at Slingsby, Ashby de la Zouche, etc.

Charter, Roll II, Edward IV

For the Lord of Hastings } The King, Archbishop, etc., greeting. Know ye that we grant license to our well-beloved and faithful William Lord Hastings, to have his houses of Ashby de la Zouche, Bagworth, Thornton and Kirby, in the County of Leicester, and his castle or house of Slingsby, in the County of York, and to build each of them with stone and lime; also to wall them, crenolate, embattle, turret and machicolate them, and to enclose and impark 3,000 acres of land and wood with the appurtenances thereof in his demesne in Ashby, and 2,000 acres of land and wood in Bagworth and Thornton, and 2,000 in Kirby, and 2,000 acres of land and wood in Slingsby; and that the said William and his heirs aforesaid have free warren in

all and each of his demesnes and woods, with all
liberties and franchise appertaining to free warren,
and that the said William and his heirs be able to
hold the said houses thus fortified, and parks thus
enclosed with warren and pasturage, himself and his
heirs in perpetuity, so that no one has a share in the
hunting in the said lands or woods or in capturing
anything therein without the license and will of
William himself or his heirs, under the penalty of
£10, so long as the lands and woods are not within
the boundary of our forest. Wherefore we wish and
affirm, etc., etc.

Given under our hand at Nottingham, 17th day of
April.

BY THE KING HIMSELF.

As there is no mention in the above
charter of a tenant in chief we may conclude that at this time Slingsby manor
was separated off from the manor of
Thirsk. Under Lord William Hastings
the castle became an important fortifica-
tion. As we shall have to speak more
fully of this remarkable personage, in the
chapter on the castle, it may be sufficient
to state here, that after his murder in
1483, all his estates were confiscated, but
shortly afterwards restored to his son
Edward, second Lord of Hastings, who

died in 1507 leaving a provision in his
will that "the manors of Welford,
Slingsby, etc., etc., should be sold to pay
his debts and perform his will" (see
"Huntingdon Peerage," Ap. E). This sale
could not have parted Slingsby manor
for any length of time from the Hastings
family, for we find Francis Hastings,
second Earl of Huntingdon, in possession
of it in 1549, in which year it passed from
him to one, John Yorke (see Ap. C).
About twelve years afterwards it was
again in the hands of the Hastings' family
in the person of Henry Hastings, third
Earl of Huntingdon (see Ap. C). Both
these men were remarkable in their way.
Francis was as close a friend of royalty
as his great-grandfather, Lord William
Hastings, had been. King Edward VI.
and he were wont to bestow costly gifts
on each other. He died 1560, and his
elaborate tomb may be seen in the church
of Ashby de la Zouche. He had six
sons and five daughters. From Edward,
his fourth son, is derived the present house

of Huntingdon. One of the five daughters was the beautiful Mary Hastings, who was sought in marriage by the Emperor of Russia, and rejected his suit. Henry, third Earl of Huntingdon, the last of the family connected with Slingsby, was a friend and loyal subject of Queen Elizabeth, who made him more than once custodian of Mary Queen of Scots, and by whose order his body was interred at Ashby with a funeral made as magnificent as possible. About thirty years before his death, *i.e.* 1563, he parted with the manor of Slingsby to a certain John Atherton (see Ap. C), of whom we have the following notice in a paper in the Castle Howard estate office entitled : "A short abstract to the title to the manors of Slingsby, Hovingham and Fryton, with observations ; purchased by Sir Charles Cavendish off John Atherton."

"It appears that Sir John Atherton was seized of a very great estate in the counties of Lancaster and Derby, and of the manors of Slingsby, Hovingham,

Fryton, and several other great estates in the county of York, and on the marriage of his eldest son John Atherton with the daughter of John Byron in pursuance to articles before marriage and by feoffment with livery indorsed dated August 10th, 15th, Elizabeth (*i.e.* 1573), the said John Atherton settled the manors of Slingsby, Hovingham and Fryton to the use of John Atherton in tail male "——" John Atherton in consideration of £7300 by feoffment of the 6 of Jan. 36 Elizabeth (*i.e.* 1594), grants the said manors of Slingsby, Hovingham and Fryton and all other lands, tenements and hereditaments in Slingsby, Hovingham and Fryton and elsewhere in the county of York of which John Atherton or Sir John his father had been in possession within 40 years——to Sir Charles Cavendish and his heirs." In this way we see how Slingsby manor passed from the family of Hastings to that of Cavendish. Of the intermediate Athertons I have been able to discover no more than is here set down : unless indeed they have some connection with John Atherton, bp. of Waterford in 1640, who was accused of an unnatural crime and being found guilty was hanged in Dublin ; his body at his own desire being buried in the obscurest part of St John's church-yard, Dublin.

THE CAVENDISHES

Camden in his description of Derbyshire traces the house of Cavendish from the ancient stock of the Gernons, one of whom is said to have owned the lordship of Cavendish in Suffolk not far from the river Stour. The first of the name of whom there is anything important to relate was Sir John Cavendish, Lord Chief Justice of the King's Bench in 1365, 1372 and 1377. He was brutally murdered by the insurgent peasantry under Jack Straw, the mob being the more incensed against him because his son John had despatched Wat Tyler after he had been stricken to the ground by the Lord Mayor : as also because of the hatred which they enter-

tained for all lawyers. "Having taken it
into their heads," writes Walsingham,
"that on all those learned in the law being
killed everything for the rest would be re-
gulated according to the decree of com-
monality; and for the future there would
be no law at all; or that if there were any,
it would be framed according to their mere
will."   In the riots of 1780 a similar
spirit was displayed, and siege was laid to
the Inns of Court with the intention of
exterminating the whole race of lawyers,
that the skin of an innocent lamb might
no longer be converted into an indictment.
The slayer of Wat Tyler had a son
William, who was a spendthrift, and sold
his landed property in Cavendish. His
grandson, Thomas Cavendish (son of his
eldest son Thomas Cavendish, who had
inherited his uncle Robert's property in
1439), was Clerk of the Pipe. He
died in 1523 leaving three sons, George,
William, and Thomas: the last died
without issue. George, the eldest, born
about 1500, was of a retiring disposition;

his name has been obscured by that of his younger and more successful brother. He served as gentleman usher to Cardinal Wolsey, continuing with him during all his successes and reverses. "He has abandoned," writes the great man, "his wife, and children, home and family, only to serve me." On the death of Wolsey, George Cavendish retired to his house at Glemsford in Suffolk, where his wife, Marjery Kemp, the niece of Sir Thomas More, lived. Here he would have doubtless ended his days in the silent seclusion congenial to his nature had he not felt constrained to take up his pen to vindicate the character of his late master "from diverse sundry surmisings and imaginary tales made of his doings and proceedings which he knew to be most untrue." This book entitled, "The life and death of Thomas Wolsey by George Cavendish," though written in 1557, could not be published at that time, owing to the unfavourable view that it took of the dissolution of

the monasteries, and the reflections that
it cast on Henry VIII. and Anne
Boleyn.   It did not actually appear till
1641.   MS. copies were, however, to be
had long before this, and it is thought
that Shakespeare may have had access to
one of these, and found in it suggestions
for his play of Henry VIII.   Certainly
the moral of the play and of the book
are one.   "Man heapeth up riches and
cannot tell who shall gather them, and
now, Lord, what is my hope? truly my
hope is even in Thee."   William Cavendish (1505-1557) was a very different
person to his brother.   For long he was
thought to be the author of Wolsey's
biography, but the finding of the auto-
graph MS. of the work signed G.C., which
is now in the B. Museum, settled the
question of authorship for ever in favour
of his brother George.   Sir William went
with the times.   He was appointed one of
the commissioners for taking the sur-
render of the monasteries—a trust which
he discharged in a manner so satisfactory

to Henry VIII. that he gave him a knight-
hood, and afterwards made him privy
councillor and treasurer of the chamber:
offices which he was pliant enough to
retain during the succeeding reigns of
Edward VI. and Queen Mary. As
might be expected his estates were enriched by large grants of land from
the dissolved religious houses, but the
greatest addition to his fortunes came
when he married Elizabeth, daughter of
John Hardwick of Hardwick Hall, Co.
Derby. Elizabeth or Bess of Hardwick,
as she is generally called, was born in
1520. Before the completion of her
fourteenth year she was a widow, having
been married at the early age of twelve
years to Robert Barley or Barlow, of Co.
Derby, whose large estates she was clever
enough even then to get settled upon
herself and her heirs. She was about
twenty-eight years old when she fascinated
Sir William Cavendish, who was so much
under her influence that he was persuaded
by her to part with all his property in the

South of England, and to purchase estates
in Derbyshire, where her own kindred
and friends lived.   She purchased the
magnificent domain of Welbeck Abbey,
and built Chatsworth at the cost of
£80,000, but before this mansion was
finished her husband died (1557).
Nothing of the building of Bess of
Hardwick can be seen to-day at Chatsworth, except the low tower near the
house called Queen Mary's bower, and
the steps up to it.   All began to be taken
down in 1687, but the work proceeded
slowly, and the last bit of the old house
was not cleared away till 1706, when the
present mansion was completed.   Judging
from the immense wages given for the mere
work of demolition, Bess of Hardwick's
house must have been marvellously well
built; there is a good picture of it at
Chatsworth.   Camden speaks of it as "a
spacious   elegant   house."   Elizabeth
Cavendish lived to bestow her hand on
a third and a fourth mate.   Her third
husband, Sir William St Lo, Captain of

the Guard to Queen Elizabeth, left everything to her at his death, to the great
detriment of his own kith and kin.

When George Talbot, sixth Earl of
Shrewsbury, her fourth husband, met her,
she was a matron of forty-six years, but
still charming. She would not be won
till the Earl had promised to further some
matrimonial schemes she had devised for
her children with certain desirable members of his family; the lover might
sigh at her feet, but "she would liever be
Bess of Hardwick again than be Countess
of Shrewsbury, if she were not to have
her own way." The Earl yielded, but
the marriage turned out unfortunately,
mainly through the worries and jealousies
consequent upon the office of custodian of
Mary Queen of Scots, conferred upon
the Earl by Queen Elizabeth. After
some years husband and wife were
separated. The bishop of Lichfield
laboured to bring about a reconciliation,
pointing out that the report that the
countess was a shrew was no just

cause of separation, for had this been
the case, "few men in England would
keep their wives long, for it was a
common jest, yet true in some sense, that
there is but one shrew in all the world,
and every man hath her, and so every
man might be rid of his wife that would
be rid of a shrew "[1] The countess survived
the Earl seventeen years.   "She was,"
writes Lodge, "a builder, a buyer and
seller of estates, a money-lender and
farmer, and a merchant of land and coals
and timber."   She acquired Bolsover
Castle, and rebuilt the ancient seat of her
ancestors at Hardwick, a few miles distant,
leaving the old house standing, "as if she
had a mind to preserve her cradle and set
it by her bed of state."   Our engraving
was made before the district was invaded by the coal trade.   It gives to the
surroundings of the Hall a sylvan aspect,
now unfortunately much changed by the
ceaseless stream of defiling smoke issuing
from the tall chimneys of Chesterfield;

[1] Lodge, vol. iii. p. 5.

but once the visitor has entered the doors
of the Hall, he forgets the gloom of
modern life, in the delight afforded by the
array of antique pictures and tapestries.
Hardwick Hall was completed about 1597;
at each extremity are lofty towers ; the
whole is lighted by eighteen windows,
each twenty feet high, and each containing
1500 panes of glass, hence the adage :—

> " Hardwick Hall,
> More glass than wall."

The main design of the building resembles
somewhat the present Slingsby Castle,
with its corner towers and huge windows,
and as Bess of Hardwick was the grandmother of Charles Cavendish, the builder
of Slingsby Castle, he may have wished to
repeat here the architectural views of his
noted ancestress. So great was the building fever on the Countess of Shrewsbury,
that the proverb was afloat that when she
ceased to build she would cease to live, and
this was actually the case, for she died
when a frost interfered with the building of
a projected large house at Owlcotes, near

Hardwick, which still stands unfinished,
a mere farm-house, now in the possession
of the Pierrepont family.

The monument of the Countess is in
All Saints, Derby, erected by herself, that
even in death she might not miss her
honours. The inscription states that she
"finished her transitory life on the 13th
day of February, in the year 1607, and
about the 87th year of her age." She had,
by Sir William Cavendish, three sons and
three daughters.   The eldest son, Henry,
died without issue (1616); the second son,
William, became Earl of Devonshire, and
ancestor of the dukes of that name; the
third and youngest son, Sir Charles, is
the first who is definitely recorded to have
had connection with Slingsby.   He purchased in 1594 from John Atherton the
manors of Slingsby, Fryton, and Hovingham, also the advowsons of Slingsby,
Fryton, and Hovingham churches.   He
had three sons.   The eldest died in
infancy, the two others, William and
Charles, were both closely connected with

Slingsby. William was patron of the living in 1662 and in 1668 (see list of rectors). The materials for his life are abundant, chiefly owing to the fact that his second wife wrote his biography. He was made Viscount Mansfield and Baron of Bolsover by James I., and by Charles I., Earl of Newcastle (1631), and afterwards Marquis. In 1638 he was appointed governor to the young prince, and there are extant two interesting letters bearing on this time — one written by Queen Henrietta Maria to her son, one of the few of her letters that have been handed down in the English tongue. She writes as follows :—

"CHARLES,—I am sore that I must begin my first letter with chiding you, but I hear you will not take physic, or I hope it was only for this day, and that to-morrow you will do it ; for if you will not I must come to you and make you take it, for it is for your health. I have given orders to my Lord Newcastle to send me word to-night, whether you will or not. I hope you will not give me the pain to go, and so I rest. HENRIETTA MARIA, R.

"To my dear son, the Prince."

The other letter is from the little prince himself, written in a child's hand, and ruled with pencil lines.   It shows the kindly relations existing between the tutor and his pupil, and the discomfort caused to the prince by his mother's propensity for dosing him.   It runs thus :—

"MY LORD,—I would not have you take too much physic, for it doth always make me worse, and I think it will do the like with you. Make haste to return to him that loves you.   CHARLES, P."
        —Jesse's "Court Memoirs," vol. iii. p. 222.

When the prince became king he rewarded his former tutor with the dukedom of Newcastle, and he himself, by his attachment to the royal cause in all its vicissitudes, is known to history as "the Loyal Duke."   On the death of his father he had succeeded to a great part of the paternal estate ; and in a survey of his properties, made in 1641, we have the manors of Slingsby, Hovingham, Fryton, Northinges, and Pomfret yielding a rent of £1700[1] out of a total annual rent

[1] "Life of the Duke of Newcastle," p. 128.

of £22,393. It seems, however, that his
brother Charles had some share in these
manors, for he built the present castle, and
in March 18, 1619, the rectory and tithes
of Hovingham were conveyed to him by
Henry Butler and Henry Ogle (C. H.
papers); but riches have wings, and both
brothers lost all after Marston Moor
(1644), which was destructive of the
royalist cause in the north. Marston
Moor is described by Cromwell in one of
his letters as " the most enormous hurly-
burly of din and smoke and steel flashings
ever seen in that time." Clarendon, who
belonged to the other party, dismisses it
in a single page, having, as he says, " no
pleasure in writing about it," and not
thinking it possible for " posterity to
receive any benefit in a more particular
relation of it "; nevertheless he describes
in detail how " the Marquis of Newcastle
and his brave brother, Sir Charles Cavendish (who was a man of the noblest and
largest mind, though the least and most
inconvenient body that lived), charged at

the head of a troop of gentlemen with as
much gallantry and courage as men could
do." These "gentlemen" were called
"Newcastle's Favourite Lambs" or
"Whitecoats"—3000 men valiant and
true, bred on the far-off moors of the
north, who earned their title of "Whitecoats" from the story that when they were
first enlisted the marquis, not having sufficient red cloth for their tunics, prayed
them to be content with white till he
could get it dyed for them ; but they
declared they desired no other, for they
would dye their coats in the blood of the
enemy. Marston Moor began unex-
pectedly at night. Prince Rupert had
told Sir William that he would not charge
till the morning, on hearing this, the
marquis had retired to his coach, which
had been drawn up at a short distance
off, and, lighting a pipe and making himself comfortable, had fallen fast asleep.
Awoke by the noise and din of battle,
and rushing into the fray, he beheld a
dismal sight—all the horse and foot of

the king's right wing in full flight, and neither his courage nor that of his brother Charles could retrieve the day. Both brothers fled to Scarboro', and there took ship for Hamburg, where they arrived on July 8th, 1644.[1]

In the following year William was in Paris, where he met Margaret, daughter of Thomas Lucas, of St John's, Colchester, who was in attendance as maid of honour to Queen Henrietta Maria. Attracted by her wit and modesty he married her (1645), and she became "the companion of his misfortunes, the solace of his exile, the sharer of his poverty." She had the pen of a ready writer, and has left matter enough to fill twelve folio volumes. Some of her writings were severely criticised. It was hinted that they were not her own, that they were deficient in learning, or that "she had plucked feathers from the universities." In the preface to her husband's biography, published in 1667, and dedicated to Charles II., she meets these

[1] "Life of William Duke of Newcastle," p. 67.

charges, and would doubtless have dealt more sharply with them had she not been commanded by her husband to mention nothing to the prejudice of any family or particular person—a command which, to satisfy her lord's generous nature, she carefully attended to. Previous to the biography of her husband she had written, in 1656, "A True Relation of my Birth, Breeding and Life," which was attached to the first edition of "Nature's Pictures, drawn by Fancy's Pencil to the Life," but immediately afterwards suppressed.

These works have received both admiration and scorn. Pepys writes, "staid at home reading a ridiculous history of my Lord Newcastle, written by his wife, which shows her to be a mad, conceited, ridiculous woman, and he an ass to suffer her to write what she wrote of him";[1] D'Israeli, in his "Curiosities of Literature," regards the duchess as a "literary wife, who was not a literary blunder"; and Charles Lamb, writing of her biography of her husband,

[1] Diary 1668, March 18th.

says : " No casket is rich enough, no cas-
ing sufficiently endurable to honour and
keep safe such a jewel." [1]

As for us in Slingsby I cannot conceive
more fascinating reading, at least for any
one caring to enter into the spirit of the
past, and to see, as it were, with the eyes
of a contemporary the kind of life lived by
the lords of Slingsby in the seventeenth
century. The duchess, speaking of her
husband's outward appearance, describes
his shape "as neat and exactly propor-
tioned, his stature of middle size." His
picture by Vandyke, engraved in vol. vi.
of Lodge's portraits, was exhibited in the
loan collection, Burlington House, 1900.
It gives him a round, well-proportioned ·
face, sandy curly hair, long taper fingers.
He wears a black coat, doublet, and hose,
with large lace collar and lace cuffs, and
a rather sad expression of countenance,
which may be accounted for by the fact
that the picture must have been taken
during his exile, for he wears the insignia

[1] " Detached Thoughts on Books."

of the garter not conferred on him till 1652. The duchess died in 1674, the duke in 1676. Their tomb, said to have been built by the duke himself, may be seen to-day in the north transept of Westminster Abbey. It is a huge monument. The duke is grasping a truncheon; the duchess holds a book with inkstand near, reminding all comers of her literary attainments, how night and day she was surrounded with young ladies who were called upon to wake at a moment's notice "to take down her grace's conceptions." Her epitaph, written by her husband, enumerates her virtues: "She was of a noble family, for all her brothers were valiant and all her sisters virtuous—a wise, wittie and learned lady, which her many bookes do well testifie. She was a most virtuous, loving and careful wife, and was with her lord all the time of his banishment and miseries, and when he came home never parted from him in his solitary retirements." Clarendon has pourtrayed the character of the duke: "He was a very fine gentleman, active and full of courage, and most accomplished in the qualities of horsemanship, dancing and fencing, which accompany good breeding in which his delight was ; besides that, he was amorous in poetry and music, and nothing could have tempted him out of those paths of pleasure, which he enjoyed in a full and ample fortune, but honour and ambition to serve the king when he saw him in distress." [1]

Amongst the duke's friends was Diepen-beck, the Dutch artist, a pupil of Rubens. He made designs for the duke's book on horsemanship, and a portrait of the duchess for her .volume of poems published in 1668 ; also a frontispiece for her " Nature's Pictures " (see plate), in which a scene is depicted that the artist may have often witnessed and enjoyed when in the employ of the duke. The duke and duchess sit crowned with laurel ; a bright log fire burns on the hearth ; one of the servants is opening a high casement window, another

[1] Clarendon's " Rebellion," bk. viii.

brings in some books ; the animated looks
and gestures of the company are meant to
convey the impression that the time is
passing swiftly ; the duchess, it may be,
recounting some of the tales which she
herself refers to as having been written
" neither to pleese or make foolish whining
lovers, but to express the sweetness of
virtue and the graces," and this is the
moral of the quaint lines underneath.
On the death of Sir Charles Cavendish,
the castle of Slingsby passed to his
nephew, Henry Cavendish, the only sur-
viving son of the loyal duke, and afterwards second duke of Newcastle (C.
H. papers).   The following letter shows
that he was well pleased with the place :—

"THE DUKE OF NEWCASTLE TO
SIR THOS. SLINGSBY.

"Wellbeck, Nov. 10th, 84 (1684).

"Noble Sir,

"I received this day yours of the 8th,
and I assure you I have a great respect for you, but
I doe not intend to sell Slingsby Castle, or any of
the £1200 a yeare I have near it.   I wounder how

this report should be yt. I was selling of it, for there was never any occasion for it. I have been soe concerned at it, I have inquired how and from whom it came; and I perceve my Lord Widdrington spoke it confidently at Gilling. I wish his Lo^p was in as good a condition as I am; sure I have served his Lo^p for these nine yeares very considerably as to his revenew. I trouble you thus much out of friendship to you, to shew there is noe such thing as my selling Slingsby.

> "I am truly,
> "Your most faithfull servant,
> "H. NEWCASTLE."

The author of the above had nine children : four sons, all of whom died in their father's life-time, and five daughters. A copy of his will in the estate office, C. Howard, dated 26th May 1691, runs as follows :—

"Henry, Duke of Newcastle, by his last will and testament, gives all his manors, etc., except Welbeck, settled on the Countess of Clare, in trust for the payment of his debts, and after payment thereof gives the revenue of all his said estate to his wife for life. And after her decease gives all his said baronies, castles, manors, mansion-houses, farms, messuages, tenancies, etc., to the Lady Margaret, Countess of Clare and her heirs, provided that the settlement be only to one child, so that his estate might remain entire and undivided, and that the heir shall take upon him or her the surname Cavendish, and for want of such issue of the said Countess, devises the said premises to the Lady Arabella Cavendish and the heirs of her body."

To the above is added :—

"It appears at Duke Henry's death the premises were subject to mortgages and debts amounting to £81,500."

According to the terms of the above will, on the death of Henry, Duke of Newcastle, the manor of Slingsby devolved upon Lady Margaret, his third daughter, who married John Holles, Earl of Clare, created Duke of Newcastle in 1694. He died in 1711, and was buried in Westminster Abbey, close to the loyal duke and his faithful duchess, in a tomb of gigantic proportions, befitting one who is described by Burnet "as the richest subject that had been in the kingdom for some ages."[1] By his will, dated 1707, "he gave all his lands in the county of York (except what he had purchased) to his only child, Lady Henrietta and her heirs, and all the

[1] "Our Own Times," vi. 62.

rest of his estate to Thomas, Duke of Newcastle" (C. H. papers). Lady Henrietta
Cavendish Holles married, in October
31, 1713, Edward Harley, afterwards
second Earl of Oxford and Mortimer.
The manors of Slingsby, Hovingham
and Fryton would be theirs, along with
the other Yorkshire estates of the Earl
of Clare, but their tenure of them was
short, for on the 12th day of September
1719 "the most noble Duke of Buckingham agreed for the absolute purchase to
him and his heirs of all the estate of the
Rt. Hon. the Lord Harley and Lady
Henrietta Cavendish Holles Harley, his
wife, in the county of York, for £28,000
and 500 guineas" (C. H. papers).

THE SHEFFIELDS

John Sheffield, Duke of Buckingham,
who purchased the manor of Slingsby in
1719, was born in 1649. He served with
honour both on sea and land in the Dutch
wars in the reign of Charles II. Though
a Protestant he went to mass with James

II., and then acquiesced in the revolution
which put that monarch from the throne,
and was created by King William, Marquis of Normanby, in the county of
Lincoln, and by Queen Anne, to whom
he made love before her marriage, Duke
of Normanby (1713), and afterwards Duke
of Buckingham.   He wrote poems and
obtained some degree of fame in this line.
Gay spoke of him as " Sheffield, who
knows to strike the lyric lyre with hands
judicious."   Addison ranked his essay on
the " Art of Poetry " with Pope's essay on
" Criticism " ; but Johnson, who has written
his life in a few pages, traces his poetic
fame to the favour and flattery of his
contemporaries, " whose criticisms were
softened by the duke's bounties and awed
by his splendours."   His name as a house-
builder will outlast his name as a verse-
builder, for it lives in the mansion which
he erected in St James' Park, which,
though now transformed into a palace,
still bears the name of " Buckingham."
In a long and pleasant letter written to

the Duke of Shrewsbury, he describes this house and his mode of living in it from which I gather the following particulars. The avenues to the house were through rows of elms, and flourishing limes, with the mall between them ; a vast town, a palace, and a magnificent cathedral were near at hand, and beyond hills and dales. Adjoining the best apartment was a greenhouse, attached to which was a closet of books, all so neatly arranged that even an Irish footman could fetch any book wanted. In the garden were the mulberry trees planted by James I. for the purpose of cultivating silkworms ; also a little wilderness of blackbirds and nightingales, and a terrace with a wall made low to admit the view of a meadow full of cattle (see plate). The place was a veritable *rus in urbe*, and the life that the duke spent therein was equally rustic and simple, for he tells us that he rose at seven in the summer, and if fine walked in his garden ; then in a spacious apartment he read and wrote. Visits could not be avoided, but, thanks to the laziness of the town, they were pretty late. After dining he drove to a place of air and exercise (*i.e.* Mary-lebone), and concluded the day in the agreeable company of his own household.[1]

The duke was three times married, and in each case to a widow. His third wife was Catherine, the natural daughter of James II. by his favourite mistress Catherine Sedley, afterwards Countess of Dorchester. She had been previously married to James Annesley, Earl of Anglesey, from whom she had been separated in consequence of the brutal treatment she had received at his hands. She was happy with the duke, for in the letter already referred to he says : "Most of my time is conjugally spent at home."

It is not to be expected that one who was daughter of the Countess of Dor-chester, and grand-daughter of Sir Charles Sedley, would be free from the vanities and foibles of the world, and the duchess had her full share of these, and seems

[1] Buckingham's "Works," vol. ii. p. 247.

to have been wanting in moral sensibility, for she delighted to call herself " Princess Buckingham"; and in a curious letter, describing her last moments, Horace Walpole writes: " Princess Buckingham is dead or dying. She has sent for the garter at arms, and settled the ceremonial of her burial. On Saturday she was so ill that she feared dying before all the pomp was come home. She said ' Why won't they send the canopy for me to see, even though the tassels are not finished.' "

John, Duke of Buckingham, died Feb. 24, 1720, a few months after the purchase of Slingsby. The duchess survived him twenty-two years, but his son and heir Edmund, the second duke, who was five years old at the time of his father's death, died under age, and without issue, of rapid consumption at Rome, Oct. 30, 1739. He left all he could to his mother, who was patron of Slingsby Church in 1739. It seems as if the first duke had a presentiment that his little son would not live long, for in his will bearing date

1716, after leaving Buckingham House to his wife, he adds, " If the testator should be so unhappy as that no legitimate son or daughter of his should live to leave that blessing of a child behind them I will and direct that Charles Herbert and his issue should have all my real estate, on condition that Charles Herbert add £500 to each of the testator's natural daughters, Sophia and Charlotte, and pay Mrs Lambert £1000 " (C. H. papers). Charles Herbert here referred to was the duke's natural son by Frances, Mrs Lambert. On the death of Edmund, he took the name of Sheffield, and succeeded to Normanby and other of the ducal estates in accordance with the will of 1716[1]; but as duke John purchased estates in the counties of York and Sussex after the making of his will, which was only altered by a slight codicil in 1717, several persons claimed to be his heirs

[1] He is buried in the chancel of the church of Burton-upon-Stather where is also an effigy of an early Sheffield temp. Edi.

and much litigation ensued which continued for many years. Among these claimants were two sisters, Margaret Daly and Magdalene Walsh, the great-great-granddaughters of Sir John Sheffield. They were contended against by Thomas Worsley and Thomas Fairfax, on the plea that " Robert Walsh, the father of the claimants, was outlawed and attainted of high treason in the third year of King William and Queen Mary, whereby all the rights that the said Magdalene Walsh and Margaret Daly could claim were devolved and vested in the King ; and his petitioners therefore most earnestly besought His Majesty that in regard that they were the nearest Protestant heirs, and in regard also that their right of inheritance was in great danger of being wrested from them by popish pretenders, that His Majesty would be graciously pleased to make a grant unto his petitioners of His Majesty's right to such real and other estate as the said Edmund, late Duke of Buckingham, died seized of "

(C. H. Papers).   The matter was finally settled by a decree of the Court of Chancery, establishing the title of Mrs Daly as heiress-at-law to John and Edmund, Dukes of Buckingham, Nov. 10, 1750.

This decision which conferred on Mrs Daly the manors of Hovingham, Slingsby, Fryton, and Wath, was materially assisted by the finding of the subjoined pedigree of the Sheffields among the papers of Duke John.   It had been corrected with his own hand, and the duchess, his widow, delivered it to Magdalene Walsh shortly before her death. (C. H. Papers.)

PEDIGREE OF WALSH FAMILY SHEWING THEIR TITLE TO THE ESTATES OF EDMUND DUKE OF BUCKINGHAM.

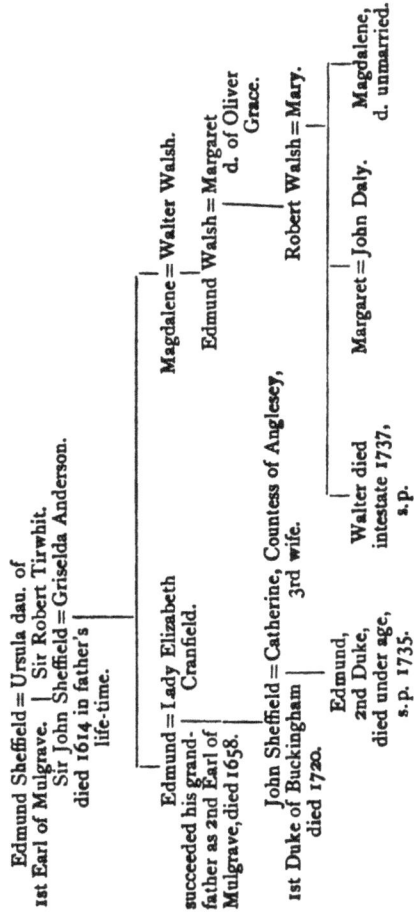

Edmund Sheffield = Ursula dau. of Sir Robert Tirwhit.
1st Earl of Mulgrave.

Sir John Sheffield = Griselda Anderson.
died 1614 in father's life-time.

Edmund = Lady Elizabeth Cranfield.
succeeded his grandfather as 2nd Earl of Mulgrave, died 1658.

John Sheffield = Catherine, Countess of Anglesey, 3rd wife.
1st Duke of Buckingham died 1720.

Edmund, 2nd Duke, died under age, s.p. 1735.

Magdalene = Walter Walsh.

Edmund Walsh = Margaret d. of Oliver Grace.

Walter died intestate 1737, s.p.

Robert Walsh = Mary.

Margaret = John Daly.

Magdalene, d. unmarried.

Mrs Daly did not long retain Slingsby, for she sold it to the Right Hon. Henry Howard, fourth Earl of Carlisle in 1751 (C. H. Papers).

THE HOWARDS

The above sale was not the beginning of the connection between Slingsby and the Howards. To trace that to its source we must go back to much earlier times. Among the noble families of the north were the Dacres of Gilsland, taking their name from the little river Dacre, on whose banks stood Dacre Castle.[1] One of these, Humphrey Dacre, was, in the reign of Richard III., made Lord Warden of the Marshes. His son, Thomas, eloped with Elizabeth Graystock, whereupon he had special livery of the lands of her inheritance,[2] which included Hynderskelf Castle, which Camden states to have been built by the Barons Greystock. Thomas Dacre died in 1525, and his grandson of the same name

[1] Camden's "Brit."   [2] Dug. "Bar.," p. 122.

married Elizabeth, second daughter of Sir James Leybourne, who outlived her husband and became the third wife of Thomas Howard, fourth Duke of Norfolk, but died shortly afterwards (1568), leaving an infant son and three daughters. The Dacre heir did not long survive his mother, being killed by an accident with a vaulting horse (1569). By his death his three sisters became co-heiresses of the Dacre lands, and their stepfather, conceived the design of uniting them in marriage with his three sons by his two former wives. Accordingly Anne, the eldest, was married to Philip, his eldest son, Earl of Arundel, and Elizabeth, the youngest, to Lord William Howard, his youngest son, who became a bridegroom at the early age of fourteen; whilst Mary, the second daughter, was intended for Thomas, Lord Howard of Walden. As Elizabeth Greystock enriched the house of Dacre, and Elizabeth Hardwick the house of Cavendish, so Elizabeth Dacre, called "Bess of the Braid Apron," from the breadth of her

possessions, enriched the house of Howard.
She brought to " Belted Will," as Lord
William Howard was called, the barony of
Gilsland and Naworth and Hynderskelf
Castle, with which last went a portion of
the manor of Slingsby (Ap. E); but
changes were frequent at these times, and
the manor of Slingsby passed in 1586 to
Thomas, Lord Howard, and the Knevetts,
his wife's relations. It was afterwards sold
by John Atherton to Sir Charles Cavendish
in 1594 (Ap. E), whose grandsons, Charles,
Viscount Mansfield, and Henry Cavendish,
together with Charles Howard, afterwards
first Earl of Carlisle, had possessions in
the place in 1655 (Enclosure Award,
C. H. Office).

Charles Howard, third Earl of Carlisle
(1669-1738), built Castle Howard on the
site of the old castle of Hynderskelf, which
had been destroyed by fire. As the
obelisk in the park records, " He likewise
made the plantations in the park, and
all the outworks, monuments, and other
plantations, belonging to this seat." The

works were begun in 1712 and finished in 1731. Lord Macaulay speaks of Castle Howard as "the most perfect specimen of the most vicious style"; but the seventh earl, in his poem on Yorkshire, fears lest

"This lyre might linger with too fond a praise
   O'er Vanburgh's airy domes and sculptur'd halls."

Arthur Young has given his impressions of the place in his "Six Months' Tour Through the North of England," published in 1770. "The castle," he writes, "is much visited by travellers on account of the great collection of antique busts, statues, and marbles it contains, and also for the beauty of the woods that surround it almost on every side. The house loses the grandeur as well as the beauty that ought to attend so large and expensive a building in the want of unity of its parts, which have as little beauty in themselves as connection with each other." Speaking of the inn, he says: "Although deficient enough in beauty, it is an excellent inn. It would be an agreeable circumstance if

travellers found the like in the neighbourhood of all great houses." In his list of
inns he adds the remark : "C. Howard,
New Inn, Crowe—An excellent house,
but dear, and a saucy landlady." Of
Hovingham Hall he writes : "The approach to Mr Worsley's house is through
a very large stone gateway, upon which
is the following inscription : — ' Virtus in
actione consistit.' Inasmuch as the building looks pretty much like the gable end
of a large house, I mistook it at first
(with that inscription) for an hospital.
Nothing should be condemned because
uncommon, but I should apprehend with
some horses that it might hazard the
necks of many a coachful if the ladies
persisted not in walking through this
approaching entrance."

Henry, the fourth Earl (1694-1758),
who purchased Slingsby from Mrs Daly
in 1751, was painted by Hudson, under
whom Reynolds studied until his greater
genius broke loose from the trammels
within which his master would have con-

fined it. The portrait is in Castle Howard, and with it may be associated those of Elizabeth Dacre and Lord William Howard by Cornelius Jansen, hanging in the dining-room — pictures somewhat dark and sombre in colour, but locally attractive to those who care to think as they look at them, that these two were the first of the Howard family connected with Slingsby.

Frederick, the fifth earl (1748-1825), succeeded when he was ten years old. He signed a bond for the payment of £25 to the overseers of Slingsby, which brings in a yearly interest of 25s. for the poor, and is one of the charities with which Slingsby is endowed.

George, the sixth earl (1773-1848), planted the avenue of trees on the *balk* at the east end of the village, and is commemorated by the east window in the church. The portrait of George William Frederick, the seventh earl (1802-1864), hangs in many of the cottages of Slingsby. It was in his time (August 1850) that

Queen Victoria and Prince Albert visited
Castle Howard, remaining two days.
The visit is still talked about. Some
old people remember how as school
children they stood on the steps of the
castle to see Her Majesty depart, and
some of a millinery turn of mind can
recall the exact bonnet she wore. It is
said that the royal children sitting at
lunch remarked that they would like to
take something away with them in remembrance of the kindness of the Earl,
and that they took four peach stones (of
which fruit they had been partaking),
washed them, wrapped them up in paper,
and said they would plant them in Balmoral.

The seventh Earl was a man of large-
hearted benevolence, keenly interested in
the welfare of the labouring classes. His
hymn on "Pray without Ceasing," com-
mencing—

> "Go when the morning shineth ;
> Go when the moon is bright,"

I have often heard quoted in the village.
As an example of his poetic skill I venture

to insert the following lines from a pamphlet found on an old book-stall, as they are not contained in the volume of the Earl's works edited by J. Gaskin :—

FOR THE MONUMENT OF ROSE, A FAVOURITE SPANIEL.

" Ye fairy sprites, who oft by dusky eve,
　When no rude noise disturbs this peaceful grove,
O'er cowslips' heads your airy dances weave,
　Or with your comrades whisper tales of love.

" A favourite's urn protect with every spell
　That by the conscious moon ye here prepare ;
Nor in the breast the heaving sigh repel,
　Nor in the redden'd eye the starting tear.

" For ye have seen her at the rise of day,
　Fair as the blushing flow'r whose name she bore,
Try the thick copse, or in the valleys play ;
　Neglect her not, tho' all her beauty's o'er.

" Lest should some heifer from the neighbouring
　　mead,
　Or playful colt her little tomb profane ;
Lest on that breast the turf too hard they tread,
　Which ne'er knew sorrow nor e'er tasted pain.

" For this may no rude peasant ere the dawn,
　With noisy rattling of their loaded teams,
Drive you with mirth unfinish'd off the lawn,
　Or in the vale disturb your pleasing dreams. "

In consequence of his duties as Lord-Lieutenant of Ireland, the seventh Earl was often absent from Castle Howard, but his brother, Lord Lanerton, loved the place, and beautified the chapel in the castle near the site of the old church of Hynderskelf, which stood just west of that corner of the house. To Slingsby Lord Lanerton was a generous benefactor, rebuilding the church mainly at his own expense. A monumental cross after the Irish pattern stands in the churchyard to his memory with the following inscription :—

"Jesu Mercy. To the glory of God.

IN MEMORY OF

ADMIRAL EDWARD HOWARD

(BARON LANERTON).

By whose piety this Church was rebuilt in 1869.

He fell asleep Oct. 8, 1880.

And so He bringeth them unto the haven where they would be."

The seventh Earl of Carlisle died unmarried, and was succeeded in 1864 by his brother William George Howard, eighth Earl and rector of Londesboro'. He also died unmarried at the advanced age of 81 in the year 1889, and was buried in the mausoleum, when his nephew, the present and ninth Earl, George James Howard succeeded to the title. To him and to Lady Carlisle I wish before closing this chapter to tender my thanks, for I have been much helped in tracing the various holders of Slingsby manor by their permission to examine the documents in the muniment room, Castle Howard. This room, a treasury of old MSS., is as fascinating to the student of history as it is delightful to the lover of nature, situated as it is amid the dark woods, broad meadows, and shining waters of Castle Howard park.

CHAPTER IV

THE WYVILLES OF SLINGSBY

Arms—Gu. three chevronels interlaced, in base vair
a chief or ; crest, a wyvern arg.

IT is not possible to give a connected
account of the Wyvilles of Slingsby ;
all we can pretend to do in this chapter is
to piece together as far as possible the
various items of information gathered from
old records as to the members of the family
who resided in Slingsby, or had in other
ways to do with the place.

The family was doubtless of Norman
extraction, and has been traced by the
Duchess of Cleveland, in her edition of
the " Battle Abbey Roll," to Guidville,
Widville or Viville in Normandy. The
name of its founder in England is stated
by various writers to have been Sir
Humphrey D'Wyville, Knight of Walworth and Slingsby Castles. There is a

Walworth Castle in Heighington Parish, not far from Darlington, which Surtees, in his history of Durham, speaks of as being "a handsome, spacious mansion, said to have been reared from its ruins in the reign of Elizabeth." But I have not been able to find that any member of the Wyville family lived in Walworth or in Slingsby in the time of the Conqueror. The nearest thing to this statement that I have been able to discover is the remark of Dugdale in his "Baronage," that " Henry I. augmented his bounty to Nigel d'Albini, the founder of the second house of Mowbray, and enfeoffed him of the vavassories of Camille and Wyville." Slingsby may have been part of the Wyville estate which in this way passed to the Mowbrays : If so, the Wyvilles continued as their sub-tenants, for we have in 34 Henry I. (*i.e.* 1130) Robert de Wyville rendering account of the farm of Roger de Mowbray (Pipe Rolls) ; and in a series of certificates made by tenants in chief of the number of knight's fees held by them, we have in the returns of Roger de Mowbray, "Richard de Wyville, 5 knights" (Liber Niger).

The first direct mention of a Wyville house in Slingsby that I have come across is in the following Patent, 17 John:

"March 20, 1215-16. Ipswich. Order from the King to Peter de Mardlay to cause Richard de Wivilee to have his house in Slingsby."

I believe this refers to the Wyville house which was afterwards Slingsby castle, and not to Wyville Hall mentioned by Dodsworth as being "in the east end of the town." Where exactly this latter building stood is a disputed point. Some identify it with the long low ivy covered house now occupied by Mr Wildsmith; others with the porched house upon the green tenanted by Mr James Hill. The following points favour the claim of this latter house. The carved oak beam over the doorway; the cellars; the fact that it was formerly part of the adjoining house on the west, and consequently once considerably larger than at present; as well as the circumstance that when the present tenant came into occupation a quantity of oak panelling existed on the walls, and was sold, as also a large old oak cabinet with the letters "I. S." and "M. W." carved above its two handsome balusters with the date "1629" in the centre. This cabinet is now in the possession of Mr Waters of Bridlington. Passing on from the reign of John we come to the Wyville whose monument is in the church (date, end of reign of Henry III.), and later on we have the William Wyville of Kirkby's Inquest (1284-85), who held $7\frac{1}{2}$ carucates of land in Slingsby under Roger de Mowbray, and was doubtless the same person as the William de Wyville mentioned in the following pleading roll, 1293.

"In the presence of Hugo de Cressingham and his fellow-justices on circuit at York in the 21st year of Edward I., William Wyvill was called upon to declare by what warrant he claimed to have free warren in all his demesne in Slingsby, Sledmere and Colton, and to have thief jurisdiction and a gallows

in Slingsby and the punishing of folk for infringe-
ment of the local market laws or rates of selling as to
beer and bread, which belonged to the Crown,
without licence or the will of his lord, the king or his
progenitors, and William Wyvill came and said that
he claimed free warren in all his demesne in the
aforesaid towns through Charter of King Henry,
father of Richard i., which had never been made
public, and he witnessed that the same King Henry
conceded to the said William that he and his heirs
should have free warren in all their lands in Slingsby,
Sledmere and Colton, so long as they were not
within the boundaries of the forest of the king, and
thief jurisdiction and gallows in Slingsby and cor-
recting of the assize of beer in the said towns, he
claimed from of old and said that he and all his
ancestors from time immemorial had used this
liberty uninterruptedly, and he made a declaration
that as to the assize of bread he had not for the
present used this.   And Roger de Hugo, who
followed on behalf of the king, said that the said
William on the right of a previous charter had taken
to himself warren in his demesne and that he abused
this liberty ; and he demanded an inquiry before the
king.   And as to his gallows and thief jurisdiction
he declared the right non-existing, and if it were
proved to exist he declared that he abused these
liberties, that he condemned thieves in his own
court beyond his fee, and he demanded an inquiry.
And he demanded also an inquiry as to the use
which he had made of his market control."

Again, we have two of this family, William and Thomas, who were important personages in Slingsby in 1300, when they contributed largely to the lay subsidy granted to Edward I. (see Ap. B). About the same time we have an Inquest post-mortem of John Wyville, 1301 A.D., which runs as follows :—

"Inquisition concerning lands and tenements which belonged to John de Wyvyl on the day in which he died, made at Sleingesby in the county of York on the feast of St Barnabas the Apostle in the 29th year of the reign of King Edward on the oath of Richard le Mareschal, Robert, etc., who declare that the said John, on the day on which he died, held certain lands and tenements in his own possession as of the fee in Slingsby, Northholm and Colton, of John, son and heir of Roger de Mowbray, under age and in the King's custody for the service of one military fee : And there is at Slingsby a certain capital messuage of the value of 20s. per ann. and no more.[1] Also there are there 18 bovates of arable land in demesne, value 5s. each per ann., total £4, 10s. od. : also in demesne 18 acres of meadow, value per acre 15d. per ann., total, 22s. 6d. : there is there no separate pasture from which the lord can receive money for the letting of the right of feeding cattle.

---

[1] This was probably the Wyville manor house, afterwards Slingsby Castle,

There are there free-holders, viz., Gilbert de Brid-
desal holding two tofts, paying per ann. at the festivals
of St Martin and Pentecost 12d.: Galfrey of Crom-
nuyl, who holds certain tofts and pays rent at same
seasons, 11d.: Galfrey le Ken, holding one toft and
croft and paying at same seasons xv^d: Hugo de
Carleton, holding one toft and paying at same seasons
11s.: Thomas de Wyvill, holding 8 bovates of land
and giving as an acknowledgment one moss rose:
and William de Yeland, holding 2 carucates of land
and giving at Easter one pair of gilt spurs. Total
rent of Freeholders of Slingsby, £5.

"There are there Bondi (*i.e.* life-tenants), who
pay rent to the said lords, each holding one toft and
two bovates of land, and paying to the said lords xx^s,
and in the time of hay harvest 11s. There are there
two Bondi, viz. Alan Melifray and Galfrid le Mound,
of whom the said Alan holds one toft and two
bovates of land, and pays to the said lords at the
feasts of St Martin and Pentecost 11s. and 8d., and
in the time of hay harvest 11s.; and Galfrid le
Mound, who holds two bovates of land, and pays to
the said lords xv^s, and in the time of hay harvest 11s.,
whether hay harvest be early or late. Total rent of
Bondi of Slingsby, £9 and 8d.

"There are also cottages there. Total rent of
cottages in Slingsby, 63s. 8d.

"There are there also two water-mills under one
roof, value per ann. 40s., and one wind-mill, value per
an. 13s. 4d. Total, 53s. 4d.

"There are there two small woods—one called Le

Fryth, value per ann. 5s., and another called Thurkel-wood, value per ann. 3s. 4d. Total, 8s. 4d.

"Also, they say that William, son of the said John, is next heir of John himself, and was twenty-six years of age at Easter last past. In testimony of which they, the said jurors, have placed their seals to this inquisition."

Again, there is a Pat. Rol. of Edward III., dated May 17th, 1336, wherein licence was granted for the alienation in mortmain to the prior and convent of Malton, *inter alia*, of three bovates of land in Slyngesby, the gift of Thomas de Wyville.

Passing on to the next century, we have a William Wyville, whose will, proved in August 14, 1430, is as follows :—

"In the name of God Amen. On the festival of St Peter ad vincula" (*i.e.* August 1st) "1430. I William Wyvill Knighte of Slingsby in Ryedale, of sound mind, leave my body to be buried in the Parish Church of Slingsby, in the midst of the same before the cross; also I leave my best saddled horse with my armour for my mortuary fee, also I leave 4lbs of wax to be burned around my body on the day of my burial with one torch; to the fabric of the Church of St Peter at York, 4 shillings and 5 pence; to each order of the Friars, at York, 2 shillings; for the altar lights of Slingsby, 4 shillings and 5 pence;

to each of my god-children, 12 pence; to my wife Agnes, I leave one house which is called Mason Place, with 4 bovates of land until the end of her life. Also I leave to Richard my son, one house, which is called Dowfecocte Place, in the southern part of the village of Slingsby. I leave to Robert my son, one house in the same village near the Cemetery, to John my son, my best 2 wheeled cart. Executors, Agnes my wife, William Wyvill my son, Edmund, Rector of Foston, and Robert Barnard Knight, my executors. Supervisors, Lord William Hastys, and John my son."

The following is the will of John Wyville, the son of the above, proved July 11, 1460 :—

" John Wyvell desires to be buried in the Choir of the Chapel of Cayton, near the body of Robert Barde, Esq. He leaves for his mortuary fee, his best horse with all his armour for his body; to the fabric of the tower of the Church of Slingsby, he gives 20s., if it may be built within 3 years after the date of his will, but if the Parishioners will not build it within that time, he leaves the 20s. to his brother, Sir William Wyvill, Rector of Dalby, to be spent on the fabric of his Church there; to John Wyvill his son and heir, 20 ewes; to Richard his son, 40s. He appoints Isabel his wife, and Sir William Wyvill his brother, his executors."

The Chapel of Cayton here referred to is

in the parish of Seamer, and has in the choir a large stone on which two brasses are fastened. One, almost square, has a shield, under which is the following inscription :—" John Wyville, of Osgodby, who departed this life 29th of January, in the year of our Lord 1705, aged 78." The other brass is a thin band, and has an inscription which is too worn to be deciphered ; but there can be little doubt that it marks the spot where John Wyville was buried in 1460. According to the terms of the above will he left, as his son and heir, another John Wyville, who must have been one of the six knights referred to by Dodsworth as having succeeded one another at Wyville Hall, the heir of whom had it on the day that Dodsworth visited Slingsby, *i.e.* July 1st, 1619, "but not," he goes on to say, "of so great estate as his ancestors were, for one of them, taking part with Stafford (that came to Scarboro' and tooke the castle), lost all his lands but only Wyville Hall, which was in jointure."

Strype, in his Memorials, gives a detailed

account of the taking of Scarboro' Castle
by Thomas Stafford in the reign of Queen
Mary, 1554 (a capture of so sudden a nature,
as to give rise to the phrase, *A Scarboro'
Warning*—meaning no warning at all,
but a sudden surprise) ; but he does not
mention the name of Wyville, although
he gives the names of all the thirty-two
prisoners taken and sent to London, as
well as the names of the thirty-one put
to death.   I am, therefore, inclined to
think that Dodsworth is really referring
to what happened seventeen years before
during the Pilgrimage of Grace, when
John de Wyville and Ralph Fenton laid
siege to Scarboro', but abandoned it at
the approach of Sir Ralph Eure, and were
afterwards taken prisoners and executed.
John Wyville, who is described as a
gentleman of £20 lands, being hanged
in chains at Scarboro', and Fenton at
York (see "Calendar of State Papers,"
February 1537).

It appears from Glover's "Visitation
of Yorkshire" (1584-85) that this John

Wyville had lands in Osgodby, near to Scarboro', where was once an old Wyville Hall, which is now a farm-house. The name of Wyville has, however, I am told, died out of the place ; but in Slingsby it will always be remembered as long at least as the castle stands, or the knight's effigy sleeps in its quiet corner in the church, or tradition keeps alive the story of the great serpent that this knight slew when he got his death's wound.

A few words on the connection between the Slingsby Wyvilles and others of the same or kindred stock may form a fitting conclusion to this chapter.

Dodsworth makes the Wyvilles of Constable Burton "descendants of the more ancient Wyvilles of Slingsby." Leland, the first of English antiquaries, writing about seventy years earlier than Dodsworth, says, "Wyvell of the north that was the ancientest of that name, had his principal house at Slyngesby in Yorkshire and this Wyvell was a man of fair landes. The house of Slyngesby and the lands of

this Wyvell be devolved to the Lords
Hastings by Heires Gen." Foster, in his
"Pedigree of the County Families," traces
Marmaduke Wyville, who represented
Ripon in 1563, to Sir Richard Wyville,
knight, slain at Towton, 1461 ; and the
said knight to that mythical personage,
for I can call him nothing else, Sir
Humphrey D'Wyville of Slingsby and
Walworth castles.

Another of the stock of Wyville with
whom the Slingsby family is said to have
been connected was Robert Wyville, the
deformed and diminutive Bishop of Salisbury. He was born at Stanton Wyville,
in Leicestershire, and was elevated in
1329 to the See of New Sarum, over
which he presided for nearly forty-six
years. It was due to his energies that
Sherborne Castle and the Bere (Bishop's
Bere) Chase in Dorsetshire were recovered to the See of Salisbury, from
which they had long been alienated. The
Bishop brought a writ of right against the
Earl of Salisbury for the recovery of the

castle. The Earl answered that he would
defend his right by single combat. On
the day of battle, the Bishop brought his
champion to the lists arrayed in white
leather, with a red surcoat of silk bearing
his lordship's arms. The Earl's champion
was arrayed and attended in a similar
fashion, his surcoat decorated with the
Earl's shield of arms. Both champions
were preparing to engage, when an order
from the King postponed the dispute.
Eventually a compromise was effected;
the castle became the property of our
Lady of Salisbury for the payment of
2500 marks. On the brass on the
Bishop's tomb in the cathedral may be
seen a representation of the castle, the
Bishop's champion, and the Bishop himself, with figures of hares in the fore-
ground, in allusion to the recovery of the
Chase of Bere. It is one of the most
perfect examples of brass engraving in
England. The epitaph records how the
Bishop, like a gallant fighter, "ut pugil
intrepidus," recovered the castle, which

had forcibly been withheld from his See for two hundred years.

Thus history endows the stock of Wyville in the person of this ecclesiastic with the same stout heart that legend attributes to the family in the person of our Slingsby knight.

CHAPTER V

IF the Sir Humphrey D'Wyvill spoken
of in the last chapter was, as it is
said, one of the Companions of the Conqueror, and Knight of the castles of
Slingsby and Walworth, then Slingsby
castle was one of the fortified places at
the time of the Conquest; but as I have
pointed out, I have failed to find the
authority for this statement. Domesday
makes the Earl of Morton and Hugh
Fitz-Baldric tenants-in-chief of Slingsby
in 1086; and Camden makes the Nevilles
the early possessors of Walworth. There
is, however, ample evidence that the
Wyvilles were early tenants of Slingsby,
and after a careful consideration of the
documents, I am led to sum up the early
history of Slingsby castle somewhat in

this way.   On the site where the castle
now stands there was originally a Wyville
castle or manor house held under the
Mowbrays, and of sufficient importance to
require a royal licence in 1216.   This
came into the hands of Ralph Hastings
in 1344, when he purchased two parts of
Slingsby manor from William Wyville.   In
the same year he had licence to crenelate,
so that then, if not before, the old Wyville
House became a castle.   This would not
break the connection between Slingsby
and the Wyvilles, for they would have
Wyville Hall in possession.   The castle
of Ralph Hastings was much strengthened
and enlarged by his grandson Lord William
Hastings in 1471.   This was the period of
the Wars of the Roses, and Lord Hastings
being an intimate friend of Edward IV. and
firm supporter of the Yorkist cause would
naturally desire to make his position in
Slingsby as strong as possible; more
especially as the neighbouring castle of
Pickering was a Lancastrian stronghold.
Hence we find he had liberty to surround

the castle with a wall (murellare), to make towers in the wall (tourellare), to pinnacle (kernellare), to embattle or make defences against assaults or sieges (imbatellare), to make holes or loops in the walls through which to shoot at assailants (turrellare), and to make a projecting gallery with openings in the floor, through which scalding water or ponderous missiles might be cast down upon the enemy (machecolare). (See chap. iii.) We can form some idea of the appearance that Slingsby Castle thus fortified and enlarged must have presented, from the moat which, on the north and west, is still in good preservation, eighty feet wide, as well as from the remains of the bailey walls. Mr Walker states in his history that at the angles of these walls once stood four turrets. The dike which runs from the beck in the direction of the castle was probably for the purpose of supplying the moat with water, and I have been told that the connection between the two was made by a leaden pipe, the end of which used to be plainly seen protruding from the grass on the inside face of the north-west corner of the moat bank. It has also been related to me that it was not an unusual thing for the Slingsby people to break off pieces of this pipe when they wanted lead. I do not vouch for the accuracy of the statement, I give it as it was given me. Certainly lead pipes are a comparatively modern invention, and water conduits in the days of Lord Hastings would be in hollowed trees, so that the pipe, if it existed at all, must have been added sometime afterwards. Not long ago the east side of the moat was still filled with water affording a pleasant skating ground for the youth of the village in winter. From the family of Hastings the Castle passed to the Athertons, one of whom, John Atherton in 1585, had it, and together with it the manor of Slingsby, when the park contained thirty-two acres of land divided out as follows : " Horse raile, six acres pasture ; the pond raile, three acres pasture; middle lawnds, three acres meadow; lower lawnds, twenty acres meadow." (C. H. Papers.) From the Athertons the manor and castle passed to the Cavendishes, one of whom was the builder of the present house. This we know from a block of marble formerly inserted into one of the front walls of the building, bearing the following inscription referred to by Eastmead in his " Rievallensis" (1824)—" This house was built by Sir Charles Cavendish, son of Sir Charles Cavendish, and brother to William Duke of Newcastle. He was a man of great virtue and learning, and died Feb. 1653, and this is placed here by order of his nephew, Henry Duke of Newcastle, in the year 1691." This stone has disappeared; the story is that one Nicholas Manners, having, as bailiff of the courts' leet and baron, the castle-yard in tenancy, took it down and converted it into a hearthstone. An old lady now dead told me that she had seen it in the house of one Matthew Etty, who lived on the Green, that Mrs Etty would clean it up that the people who came from visiting the castle might read the inscription. She also told me that Nicholas Manners was an only child, that his mother lost her husband when she was young, that she was engaged a second time, but on going to church the bridegroom was nowhere to be seen and never came, which so affected her that she went home and died.

This is not the only instance in the annals of Slingsby of defaulting bridegrooms. Tradition tells of one, who on the eve of the wedding-day visited the bride with a fine, fat goose for the wedding breakfast; and then to the unfeigned astonishment of all, was not present to partake of the good fare he had provided. He left the goose to make his apologies. It is pleasant to relate that the expectant bride on this occasion did not shed idle tears upon the vagabond, but shortly afterwards consoled herself with a worthier mate.

The exact date of the building of the

Cavendish house is difficult to discover. It could scarcely have been built before 1619, for in that year Dodsworth noted a maunch (the Hastings' crest) over the gates : and "the walls of a fine chapel nere as big as the church within the castle walls," of which there are no traces in the present ruins ; nor could it have been built after 1644, for in that year Sir Charles Cavendish fled from England along with his brother the loyal Duke ("Life of Duke of Newcastle," p. 37). If we place the building in the year 1640, we shall not be far wrong ; and this is the date assigned to it in Mr Walker's history. The local tradition that Sir Charles never finished his house is borne out by the appearance of the ruins ; the green mounds on the sward to the south and east when dug into are found to be full of stone chippings and such-like débris, suggesting that the masons were hastily called away before they had finished their task. This would seem to confirm the idea that the time of the building was about

1640 when the country was greatly disturbed, and loyal supporters of Charles
I. as were the Cavendishes, would have
little time for domestic architecture.   I
have questioned the oldest inhabitants of
the village, who can remember as far back
as 1820, and I have never come across
anyone who can recall the time when the
castle was anything but a ruin; and yet
what remains of it is so substantially built,
that had it been completed, it could
scarcely have had time to fall into its
present dilapidated condition,[1] unless,
indeed, it was partially destroyed in the
time of the Commonwealth, as Bolsover
Castle, another of Sir Charles' possessions
certainly was; for on his compounding
for it, he found that a purchaser had
pulled down much of the building with
the idea of making money out of the

[1] The following entry made in the registration of
papist estates, June 29, 1749, proves that the castle at
that date was a complete ruin : "Margaret Daly the
manor of Slingsby, wherein is a ruined house called
Slingsby castle, untenanted and of no value." N.R.
Records, vol. viii. p. 17.

material (" Life of William, Duke of New-castle," p. 94). Enough remains, however, of Sir Charles' house to show that he intended to have in Slingsby a mansion worthy of his name, and of the architectural fervour of his grandmother Elizabeth Hardwick; indeed, Hardwick Hall and Slingsby Castle have many features in common; specially are we reminded of the former, when we look at the large windows of our castle, some of them twelve feet high by seven feet wide. I am indebted to Mr Reavel, late clerk of Castle Howard, for a ground plan of the castle,[1] from which it may be seen that the first or basement story consists of two large rooms flanked east and west by smaller rooms, probably intended for cellars, store-rooms, and such-like, with octagon pillars in the western rooms supporting the roof. One of the two larger rooms was a kitchen, with two immense fireplaces, each 12 feet wide. A similar arrangement characterises the second story. A third

[1] See plate.

story was intended. The fireplaces are a prominent feature of the house, giving the impression that Sir Charles was as fond of heat as of light. Projecting portions of the walls of the two towers mentioned by Mr Walker in his history as being on the east ánd west, and 23 feet square, still remain. The east tower probably formed the chief entrance. A very peculiar feature of the castle are the twelve small rooms, one at each corner on each story (R. R. in plan). The block plan is meant to represent the surroundings of Lord Hastings' castle when the moat and bailey walls were intact. As to the designer of the house, it is hard to say who it is likely to have been. It may have been Huntingdon Smithson, whose father worked with the noted architect or builder, John Thorpe, a variety of whose plans may be seen in the Soane Museum, London. John Thorpe built Wollaton, which is not unlike Slingsby in design. The Rev. George Hall, in his history of Chesterfield (1823), states that "on a

stone in the building, on the west side of
Bolsover Castle, is engraved 'H. S.,
1629,' meaning no doubt Huntingdon
Smithson," and as Bolsover Castle belonged to the Cavendishes, they may have
employed the same architect for their
Slingsby house. Some of the stone of
which the castle is built is a kind of freestone; it probably came from a quarry
in the lower calcareous grit, the site of
which may still be traced on the entrenchment upon Slingsby Bank wood. The
castle has suffered from the hand of man
as well as from the effects of time. Many
of the carved stones were taken to build
the cellars of the rectory, where they may
still be seen. "The west front of the
rectory house," writes Mr Walker, "which
is more modern than the other part of the
building, bears many decided evidences of
being composed of materials pillaged from
the castle, taken, it is said, from the west
tower, which must have been destroyed at
no distant date from its erection, as one
of the windows of this part of the rectory

bears the date 1740." One of the inner
walls of the castle is despoiled of its surface
stones, which, tradition says, were removed
to build an additional story to the rectory,
until one of the Lords of Carlisle, hearing
of the matter, put a stop to this piece of
vandalism.   Nor is it alone the rectory
that has benefited at the expense of the
castle.   Many of the cottages in the
village have been furnished with building
material from the same source.   About
eighty years ago—so I am told—the castle
had in one of its rooms a *shilling mill*, or
mill for shilling or shelling oats.   The oats,
which were brought in great quantities
from the surrounding neighbourhood, were
then spread upon a perforated tile floor,
the under side of which was fashioned into
a number of small square tubes with the
object of drawing up the flame of the fires
which were lit underneath.   The oats,
when dried, were separated by machinery
from their husks, and eventually turned
into oatmeal for stock.   This was when
water still filled the eastern side of the

moat, for I am told that it was the shooting of the husks into the water which led to the filling up of the moat at this point and making it profitable as a garden or orchard, as it is now. There was also in old time in one of the rooms of the castle a bakehouse, where the villagers baked their bread, and the oaten husks were often used for kindling. The hole in the roof, where the chimney of the oven passed through, may be still seen in the room in the south-west corner.

It is the lament of some that the records of the past have so little to say of Slingsby Castle. It is true we hear of no tragedy occurring within its walls to excite the imagination or curdle up the blood ; but to those who are content with less piquant fare the fact that it was under the overlordship of the Mowbrays for many years is in itself quite sufficient to surround the place with considerable historic interest. The Mowbrays were great barons, renowned in peace and war, and their tenancy of Slingsby connects the place with the whole neighbourhood, and with the events which were happening therein.   Sir Roger de Mowbray presented to the canons of Newboro' Priory no less than seven churches, and amongst these the church of Hovingham.   The neighbouring townships of Fryton and Wath were his, as parts of his manor of Hovingham.   In Fryton he had six carucates of land, whereof John de Barton held three and Matthew de Levain two. In Wath he had one carucate, held by Nicholas de Stapelton.   Both these places were ecclesiastically important.   Wath had a religious house for women, the traces of which may still be seen on the high ground above the mill.   Fryton had a chapel endowed with one oxgang not geldable.   We learn from the same source whence the above statements are taken, *i.e.* Torres MSS., that "a certain controversy happened between the prior and convent of Newborough on one point and Richard de Barton, Esq., Lord of Fryton, on the other, touching the finding of a

chapleyne to celebrate mass, etc., in the
chapel of Fryton, which was thus composed, viz. "that the lords prior of the
convent and their successors shall, for the
term of ninety years ensuing, find to the
Lord Richard, his heirs, and assigns to
all the inhabitants of the town of Fryton
a certain chaplain daily to celebrate masse
in the same chapel, and for this grant per
concordiam the Lord Richard and his
heirs Lords of Fryton shall pay to the
said chaplein for the time being, in
augmentation of his portion, £26, 8s. 0d.
per ann." The castle well may be assigned
to Mowbray days, for as soon as a castle
was built a good well would be a necessity, and this is an excellent source of
water that has never been known to fail.
The "Mowbray" oak, situated in the
Priest's Park, although scarcely dating
back to so far distant a time, has at least
in its name a reminder of the same family.
When Mr Walker measured this tree in
1845 it was 17 feet in circumference,
7 feet from the ground; now, in 1903.

measured at the same point, it is 18 feet.
The tree is evidently in its declining days.
About thirty years ago it was struck by
lightning, and the scar has lately been
brought to light by the woodpeckers, who
have picked off the overgrowth of bark in
their search for insects.   In this field may
be gathered fine specimens of the adder's
tongue fern.

Additional historical interest is given to
the castle, when we think of it in the hands
of Lord William Hastings.   He was
one of the foremost men of the time.   His
moral character has somewhat suffered
from his intrigues with the beautiful and
unfortunate Jane Shore; and the suspicion
that he had a part in the murder of young
Prince Edward after the battle of Tewkes-
bury has left a dark stain upon his
memory; but, apart from these things,
he was a man who has earned the praise
of many.   Dugdale gives a list of eighty-
one persons retained by him in peace
and war : among whom we have the
name of Robert Slyngesby, Esq.   Fuller

writes of him : " The reader needeth
not my dim candle to direct him to
the illustrious personage whom King
Edward IV., or rather Edward Planta-
genet (because more in human than in
royal capacity) so delighted in." Sir
Thos. More, in his history of Richard
III., passes upon him the following eulo-
gium : " Lord Hastings was an honourable
man, a good knight, and a gentle, of living
somewhat dissolute, plain and open to his
enemy, and sweet to his friend ; easy to
be beguiled as he that forestalled no peril ;
a loving man and passing well-beloved,
very faithful and trusty, and trusting too
much." Under the control of such a lord,
the dwellers on the manor of Slingsby
would be kept in touch with the great
world, and the doings of their chief would
be the talk of the place. As master of
the mints in Calais and London Lord
Hastings introduced the " noble " into
England, a gold coin of the value of 8s. 4d.
He accompanied Edward IV. in his expedition planned for the conquest of France

in 1475. It took three weeks to transport the English troops across the Straits of Dover. They returned without striking a blow. Louis XI. had no intention of risking a battle. He cajoled Edward by means of bribes and flattery. At one time it was three hundred cartloads of the best wines of the country which the King of France sent to his cousin the King of England. At another time it was a present of plate, value 10,000 marks, which he sent to my Lord Hastings. At last the two monarchs met at Picquigny near Amiens, on a bridge thrown across the Somme, there being a barricade between them, for Louis was very suspicious; the King of England bowed low on one side and Louis, who was leaning against the barrier on the other side, hating Edward in his heart but full of trepidation and anxiety, bowed in like manner and said, " Cousin, you are right welcome; there was no person living I was so ambitious of seeing, and God be thanked that this interview is on so good

an occasion;" the King of England returned the compliment in good French,
and a treaty was drawn up, and Louis
agreed to pay to the English king 75,000
crowns at once and an annuity of 50,000
crowns, besides pensions to certain of the
English nobility. All this is amusingly
told by Philip de Commines, who adds
that it was through his influence that
Lord Hastings was persuaded to become
one of the French King's beneficiaries.
Louis promised him an annuity of 2000
crowns; but Lord Hastings refused on
the first payment of the money to give a
receipt, saying, to the messenger that
brought it, "this present proceeds from
your master's generosity, not from any
request of mine; if you have a mind
that I should receive it, you may put
it into my sleeve, but neither letter
or acquittance will you have from me,
for it shall never be said of me
that the High Chamberlain of England
was pensioner to the King of France;
nor shall my receipt ever be produced

in his chamber of accounts." We might have credited this transaction with being the origin of the maunch or sleeve charged upon the shield of the Hastings family, and seen by Dodsworth engraven on the Slingsby church steeple, had we not evidence of its existence in earlier times, as for instance, on the cross of John Hastings, Earl of Pembroke in Elsyng Church, Norfolk (1347). The death of Edward IV. in April 9, 1483, deprived Lord Hastings of his best friend and protector ; and he himself was shortly afterwards cruelly slain by Richard III. Shakespeare makes this an act of retribution for the murder of Prince Edward, and conjures up before the mind of Hastings as he is hurried from the Tower to his death, the form of the distracted and vengeful mother.

"Oh, Margaret Margaret, now thy heavy curse
Is lighted on poor Hastings' wretched head."

It has been thought by some, and it is at all events a pretty fancy, that this tragic incident is accountable for the change which took place in the Hastings' arms. The family originally carried a red sleeve upon a gold ground, but afterwards a black (sable) sleeve on a white (argent) ground. The remains of Lord Hastings were buried in the north aisle of St George's, Windsor, in a small chapel built in memory of her husband by Catherine, his widow, the sister of the Earl of Warwick. The chapel adjoins the tomb of Edward IV. and is dedicated to St Stephen, whose history is painted on the four inside panels.

Of all that was once the Castle of Hastings in Slingsby there is now nothing to be seen except the moat, the remains of the bailey walls, and perhaps the vaults and substructions, so completely was the castle transformed into a modern house by Sir Charles Cavendish.

In the life of the Duchess of Newcastle, written by herself, we have some details as to Sir Charles. The portrait is a most attractive one. We see him and his brother

united in more than a brotherly union.
Their father early perceived the difference
in their characters, and let each follow the
bent of his genius. William was a lover
of sport and horses, but Charles was more
attached to books ; but this variety of
temperament only quickened the love they
had for one another.   They shared each
other's joys, and poverty and misfortune
only drew them closer together. By reason
of the weakness of his body Charles had
no command at Marston Moor ; but he
stayed by his brother during the whole of
the battle, and they fled together afterwards to Hamburgh. When Duke William
was reduced to great straits for money, he
sent his wife to England to see if she could
obtain from Parliament what was usually
allowed to the wives of delinquents out of
the estates of their husbands.   Sir Charles
accompanied her ; and Lady Newcastle
gives a detailed account of how she
occupied her time in town. She seldom
stirred out of her lodgings except to pay
a few visits, or to take an airing with her

sisters in Hyde Park. The only recreation she seems to have given herself was
to go three or four times to hear music in
the house of one Mr Lawes. Hereby
may hang a tale. Mr Lawes was Vicar-
Choral of Canterbury Cathedral. He composed the music for Comus, and acted in
it the part of Thyrsis and the attendant
spirit. He is celebrated by Milton in one
of his sonnets, and it may be that on one
or more occasions when Sir Charles and
Lady Newcastle were present at his house,
the great puritan may also have been there,
and the lady royalist and the defender of
the Commonwealth may have met and
sunk their differences as they listened to
the "soft pipings" and "smooth ditties"
of a mutual friend. The main object of
Lady Newcastle's visit to England was of
no avail. Lord Lucas, her brother, brought
her claims before the Committee, but he
was told that nothing could be allowed her
by reason of her marriage having taken
place after her lord's delinquency, as also
because he was an "arch-traitor" to the

State.   Lady Newcastle, who was present
in the court, would hear no more.   She,
"whispering, spake to her brother to con-
duct her out of that ungentlemanly place."
And as this was the first committee she
attended, so it was the last, for she found
"their hearts as hard as her fortunes, and
their natures as cruel as her miseries."   It
is right, however, to add that the severity
of Parliament did not extend to the Duke's
daughters, who were allowed to remain in
England ; and a letter of theirs thanking
Lord Fairfax for his favour and protection,
is contained in the Fairfax correspondence
(iii. 194).   Sir Charles, too, was per-
mitted to compound for his estates for the
sum of £5000, out of which sum he sent
relief to his brother.   After a year and a
half in England Lady Newcastle returned
to her husband, leaving Sir Charles sick
of an ague, of which sickness he died (*i.e.*
1653-4, about the age of sixty-three).
"Heaven knows," she writes, "I did not
think his life was so near an end, for
his doctor had great hopes of his

perfect recovery; but not being of a
strong constitution, he could not, as
it did prove, recover his health, for
the dregs of his ague did put out the
lamp of his life." And then she
breaks out into this rhapsody: "I will
build his monument of truth, tho' I cannot of marble, and hang my tears and
scutchions on his tomb. He was nobly
generous, wisely valiant, naturally civil,
honestly kind, truly loving, virtuously tem-
perate. His promise was like a fixt
decree; his words were destiny; his life
was holy; his disposition mild; his be-
haviour courteous; his discourse pleasing.
He had a ready wit and a spacious knowledge, a settled judgment, a clear under-
standing, a rational insight. He was
learned in all arts and sciences, but specially in mathematicks, in which study he
spent most part of his time; and though
his tongue preached not moral philosophy,
yet his life taught it; indeed, he was such
a person that he might have been a pattern
for all mankind to take. He loved my lord

his brother with a doting affection, as my lord did him." Make what deduction we like from these encomiums for the excessive partiality of affection, enough remains to assure us that Sir Charles must have been a most lovable and distinguished personage ; a conclusion confirmed by two letters written by Sir Edward Hyde to Secretary Nicholas, in one of which, dated Antwerp, November 1651, he writes : "My Lady of Newcastle ventures thither this week with Sir Charles Cavendish, as well to urge some deeds of trust which he hath long been in for his brother, as to endeavour to enjoy the benefit of the composition which was made long since for his own estate. I hope he will have some good fruit of his journey, for truly he is one of the worthiest persons and the best Christian that I know." In the other letter, dated Paris, March 1653-4, he says : "You have heard of the sudden death of the Earl of Shrewsbury, and as sudden of worthy Sir Charles Cavendish, who cannot be enough lamented, as one of the most excellent persons the world had, of the greatest virtue and piety. I fear his brother will find it an irreparable loss to him, who surely very much subsisted by his kindness." [Clarendon State Papers.]

It may be that what has been here said of Sir Charles Cavendish and his predecessors, may tend to increase the interest of the castle ; for my part I have felt that it adds considerably to the charm of the place and its surroundings to be able to people it with the denizens of the past. The illustrations which we give are from photographs, by Mr Crowther, curator of the Leeds Museum ; and were taken from the south, and from the north-west corner of the castle. It may not be an unfitting conclusion to this chapter to observe that this ruined mansion has been a dear neighbour to me for many years. I have looked upon it from the elevation of the Malton Road when the rays of the autumn setting sun shone through its great windows flooding the village with golden light. I have loitered on a summer's day beneath its ivy-mantled walls, and heard the jack-daws from its summits expostulating with my human interference with their privacy. I have watched the sparrows nesting in its nooks and corners, with the pigeons flying high above its towers and taking the sunlight on their wings. I have passed the pile at midnight when the starlings were still busy "striking their tiny castanets," and at these and all other times, I have felt the wish that its beauties and its history were more widely known.

CHAPTER VI

THE CHURCH AND RECTORS

SLINGSBY church is one of the eight churches in the deanery of Helmsley dedicated to All Saints, but the village feast is not on All Saints' Day, November 1st, but on the 13th and 14th of May, which is curious as we expect the church dedication festival and the village feast to tally. In reference to this it may be worth while to point out that All Saints' Day was originally May 1st (*i.e.* May 13th, new style), and that it was not till 834 A.D. that it was transferred by Pope Gregory IV. to November 1st. This might seem to suggest that there was a church in Slingsby in very early times, but we must remember that the place is not Anglian but Danish, and that it was not till the latter half of the ninth century that the

168

Danes came as settlers, and even then they came as heathen and remained such for many years, and the last thing that Eslinc would think of doing would be the erection of a Christian place of worship. But although we cannot assign to Slingsby an early pre-Norman church we may safely say that one was in existence before 1086 for Domesday records of the manor, "there is a priest *there* at present," and a priest may be considered as implying a church. The church is first directly mentioned in the Whitby Cartulary, where it is referred to in no less than eight charters. Charter No. 1, "a memorial of benefactions," certainly of a date anterior to 1175 A.D., has the following, "By the gift of William Hai and Robert Chambord the church of Slingsby." In charter No. 45, "Roger Abp. of York" (*circ.* 1154-1190), "confirms to the monastery and monks of Whitby the church of Slingsby." Charter No. 90 contains the following, "Be it known to all sons of Mother Church, that I, Robert

Chambord, for my salvation, and for the souls of my father and mother, and of all my predecessors hath given and by this, my present charter hath confirmed to God and St Peter, and the holy St Hilda of Whitby and to the monks serving God there, as a free and perpetual alms, the church of Slingsby, reserving the tenure of Samson Clerk so long as he shall live and continue in a secular habit. This same Samson Clerk of Slingsby being present at the time, and among others freely approving of the donation." In charter No. 91 we have, "Masci de Curci, with the assent of his wife Matilda, and Richard, his son, confirming to the monks of Whitby, Slingsby church, according to the grant originally made by William Hai." Charter 194 is a royal charter of Henry II., which confirms to Whitby Monastery the church of Slingsby, according to the deed of Robert Chambord. Charter No. 300 bears date 22nd day of August 1363, and is a deed in which "John Thoresbi, Archbishop of York

(1352-1374), confirms to Whitby the
pension of 13s. 4d., payable from Slingsby
church." Charter No. 335 is an agreement made in the King's Court, York, in
the 4th year of the reign of King John,
in the presence of John, Bishop of
Norwich (1200-1214), between William
Chambord, petitioner, and Peter, Abbot of
Whitby, to the effect that the said William
Chambord remitted all right and claim
which he had in the advowson of Slingsby
church to Peter, Abbot, and his successors
and for this, Peter, Abbot, gave to the said
William Chambord, 5 silver marks.

Charter 394 is dated 13th day of June
1515, the seventh year of Henry VIII.,
and is a presentation of the advowson and
right of patronage of Slingsby church to
Brian Darlay, Professor of Divinity, and
George Evers, Public Notary, "for one
and the next turn only." This charter
was made 497 years after the date of the
death of Reinfrid, the first prior, and
25 years before the dissolution of the
Monastery, in the reign of Henry Deval,

the last Abbot. He surrendered Whitby
Abbey into the King's hands in the year
1540, only covenanting for the settlement
of some small pensions on the Monks
during life, or until they were otherwise
provided for in the church.

It appears from these charters that the
church of Slingsby was given by William
Hai, and John Chambord to Whitby
Abbey, before 1175, and that the patronage was in the hands of the monks for at
least 365 years.

The pension of 13s. 4d. mentioned in
charter No. 300 is still one of the out-
goings of the rectory, and is paid under
the name of fee-farm-rent to the officer of
Messrs Danby & Bamber. It is interesting to trace the steps through which this
money payment has passed. On the
dissolution of the monasteries, all lands,
tithes, rents, pensions, etc., belonging
to the monasteries passed into the hands
of the Crown, and Henry VIII. had power
to grant them away through the court of
Augmentation ; but in the time of Charles

I. there still remained in royal hands a great amount of these properties, which had not been given away, or had reverted to the Crown. These naturally passed on the death of Charles to the Commonwealth parliament. In 1649, and the following years, acts for their sale were passed, but the times were insecure and few were sold. After the restoration, in order to stimulate the desire to purchase, an act was passed in 1670 (22 and 23, Ch. II., c. 24), giving full guarantee for the safety of these properties as investments, and vesting the special powers of the Crown as to collection and recovery in the purchasers and their successors. Under this act the Slingsby pension was sold, and is mentioned among a great mass of other properties in an indenture of sale bearing date August 12th, 1672 (Public Record Office). It is now the property of Mr Gosling, the successor in title to the original purchaser. A fee-farm-rent, it may be observed, is, as its name indicates, a rent charge on land that has been let, or farmed out, to a tenant in fee, *i.e.* in perpetuity, but on condition of the rent charge being paid.

Additional notices of Slingsby church are to be found in the following : (1) In Kirkby's Inquest, 1284 (see Ap. A); (2) in Pope Nicholas' taxation (1291); (3) in the New Taxation (1318); (4) in the Inquisition Nonarum ; and (5) in the Valor Ecclesiasticus or Liber Regis (1534), which transferred the first fruits and tenths from Rome to the King ; where the Slingsby benefice stands at £12, 1s. 10d. In 1703 Queen Anne parted with her right to these subsidies, and they have ever since been paid to the office of Queen Anne's Bounty for the increase of the value of smaller livings. On my institution I paid as first fruits £12, 1s. 10d. and as tenths I now transmit yearly to the same office 24s.

When the foundations for the new church were being digged, a great number of skulls were found under the wall of the south aisle, suggesting that

this part of the ground was originally
churchyard, and that the old Norman edifice consisted of no more than
chancel and nave, the aisles being added
afterwards—first the north, and then the
south, as was usual. It appears from
the report of the architects, Messrs Austen
and Johnson of Newcastle, who rebuilt the
church in 1867, that towards the close of
the fifteenth century extensive alterations
had been made in the old church, in-
cluding the erection of a clerestory and
tower, and the rebuilding of the aisle
walls ; that the chancel arch was of the
same date, and that the chancel probably
shared in the general recasting the church
underwent at that time ; though this was
declared to be uncertain owing to the
chancel having been rebuilt in a most
incongruous manner in 1835. The
report further stated that the whole
building was in a very insecure condition,
the bases and some of the capitals of the
pillars being crushed and split by the
superincumbent weight, and the pillars

very much out of the perpendicular, the arches consequently much depressed, whilst the upper part of the tower, shattered in every direction and bound together by iron ties, had been so pieced and patched that it was in a dangerous state; consequently the architects felt compelled to recommend that the church should be entirely taken down and rebuilt.

With this description of the old church may be compared two others: that given in Mr Walker's " Brief Account of Slingsby," written in 1845; and that given in Sir Stephen Glynn's " Notes on Yorkshire Churches." Mr Walker writes as follows :—

" The church is a neat and commodious building, containing 400 sittings open to all. The more ancient parts consist of Norman pillars of the twelfth century, and there are many remains of Norman gravestones, but the original building has suffered much from time and other causes. All the outer walls have at different times been rebuilt in various styles of architecture ; it has also been substantially re-roofed, and recently covered with Welsh slates. The fine massive tower contains three good bells : it appears to be of the late Tudor style. The church now consists of a western tower, a chancel which was entirely re-built in 1835, a nave with clerestory windows, and north and south aisles. On the east end of each aisle there appears to have been formerly a chapel. The entrance from the nave is by a handsome pointed arch, and a similar arch opens into the tower."

Sir Stephen Glynn visited Slingsby, Nov. 19, 1863. The following notes taken by him on this occasion have been furnished me by the Rev. Dr Cox :—

" The church (All Saints') has clerestoried nave, with N. and S. aisles, chancel with N. and S. aisles or chapels. West tower and S. porch. The N. aisle is narrow, the nave is rather short, and divided from each aisle by two pointed arches, those on the N. are pointed, and good EE. upon tall circular column, with moulded capital. On the S. the arches are plainer and shorter, but also EE., and the most western arch is cut off by the curious arrangement of the present porch, which is formed within the aisle, and is actually its western portion inclosed.

"The N.E. respond is a corbel on foliage. The north aisle has square headed windows of two lights and Perpr. Those on the S. have been mostly mutilated. The clerestory has square headed windows of two lights. The tower arch is plain pointed. The chancel arch is pointed, springing at once from the wall. There is a pointed arch separating the

S. aisle of the nave from that of the chancel. The chancel has a new roof, and extends beyond both aisles. It is divided from the N. chapel by one arch of flat and depressed form—from the S. chapel by one straight sided and wide arch. The north arch is on imposts of EE. foliage; the S. arch on plainly moulded imposts. The E. window of the chancel is a poor pointed one of three lights. At the E. end of the S. aisle appears a vesica-like opening, now walled up. The other windows of this chapel are square headed, of two lights. The interior of the nave has several plain old open benches with knobs on the ends, of about Charles I. period. The tower is Perpr.—has parapet and corner buttresses—and a slightly gabled roof. There are two string courses, a W. window of three lights, and square headed labeled belfry windows of two lights.

"The clerestory has a new slated roof. The N. aisle has no parapet, but the S. aisle has one. The porch has its windows unglazed; the inner doorway has an ancient door, with tracery in wood."

Neither Sir Stephen Glynn nor Mr Walker make any mention of the west gallery, but reference is made to it in the report of the architects. Here the musicians sat, who with flutes, violins, clarionets, and a violoncello accompanied the singing. The introduction of an harmonium and afterwards of an organ put

an end to this. The old church began
to be pulled down on old May-day 1867,
and the foundation stone of the new
building was laid by the Hon. Mrs Howard
on Sept. 24 in the same year. It was
an oblong block of the Appleton Oolitic
freestone. In the cavity below the stone
were deposited a bottle hermetically sealed,
containing a record on parchment of the
demolition of the old church, and the in-
cidents leading to the erection of the new
one, with the names of the patron, rector,
architect, and builder; also a newspaper of
that day's date, and some of the current
coins. The greatest care was taken to
preserve, as far as possible, the architectural features of the older building, and
whatever old relics the church contained.
The cost of the rebuilding was about
£5000, the greater portion of which was
borne by the Hon. Admiral Howard.
Among the remains of the old church still
preserved may be noticed some old stones
with incised crosses let into the outside
wall of the tower, probably dating from the

thirteenth century; part of the pillars on the north side of the nave; a memorial brass to Sir John Fons, one of the rectors; some flat-tombstones, together with that which is our most interesting relic, the effigy of a knight, one of the Wyvilles, which Dodsworth refers to in his notes (see Ap. D.). The talbot has disappeared from the feet of the effigy, and the legs of the knight have been broken off, and the charge upon the shield is no longer seen—otherwise the monument, which lies in the same position as it did in the old church, is in excellent preservation; the chain-mail is beautifully finished; the heart lies within the hands uplifted in prayer; the surcoat is cut up the middle, indicating transition to the cyclas; and the sword-belt hangs to the girdle not by one, as was usual in earlier times, but by two points of attachment—features which go to fix the date of the monument as belonging to the latter part of the reign of Henry III. Although the connection between cross - legged effigies and the crusades has lately been pronounced a mere fond imagination, there is a tradition that this Wyville was a crusader, in which case he may have taken part in the ninth and last crusade set on foot by Louis I X., and joined after the Battle of Evesham by Prince Edward and 150 English knights.

" 'There is a tradition,' writes Dodsworth, continuing his notice of this monument, 'that betwixt Malton and this towne ther was sometymes a serpent that lyved upon prey of passengers, which this Wyvill and dogg did kill, wher he received his deathes wound. There is a great hole, half a myle from the towne, round within and 3 yerdes broad and more wher this serpent lay, in which tyme the street was turned a myle on the south side, which doth still show itt self if any take paynes to search itt.' "

There are difficulties arising out of these statements of Dodsworth, for the hole which is now known as the serpent's hole is twenty-one yards broad by eighteen yards long, and fully a mile from the town. It is situated on the southern edge of Low Pot Close, and in such a position

that a turning of the Malton Road to the
south would be turning the road *towards*,
and not away, from the lair of the serpent ;
but by the street that was turned Dodsworth may have meant not the Malton
Road but the trackway by the entrenchment, which in East-thorpe Bank wood *is*
turned to the south and *away* from the
serpent's hole. Descending from the
realms of imagination and regarding the
serpent's hole from the standpoint of
prosaic history, there can be little doubt
about what it really is. It is an old disused limestone quarry, not a disused
gravel-pit as it is designated in the
ordinance survey map, as there is no
gravel at all in the limestone, and the
elipse-like depression scooped out of its
N.E. flank was no doubt the clamp, or
place within the quarry, where the lime
was burnt. The whole presents to-day
the appearance of a cup-like hollow on
the hill-side, lined with green grass and
starred in spring with innumerable violets,
anemones, primroses and cowslips, for

there is no spot in the parish where wild flowers grow in greater beauty and profusion, or the lark when the sky is blue sings a lovelier song.

Next to the Wyville monument is a flat tombstone seven feet long by two feet three inches broad at the top, tapering to one foot nine inches broad at the bottom. It bears a foliated cross in relief, the head treated in the conventional fashion which prevailed throughout most of the thirteenth century, whilst the stem is treated naturally, narrowing upward from the base, and having on each side four branches. It stands on a calvary of three steps. When the church was being rebuilt a skeleton was found underneath this slab enclosed in a stone coffin, also a massive gold ring having a death's head and cross-bones in solid gold set in white enamel in the middle, with blue enamel at the sides. A portion of the white enamel crumbled away on being exposed to the air. The ring was not re-interred, but given to Lord Lanerton for the museum at Castle

Howard, but where it is now no one seems to know. Next to the cross-slab is a plain flat stone, once the top of the side altar which stood here in old days, for two incised crosses may still be seen at two of the corners. The church contains some fine stained glass windows by Clayton and Bell. A Jesse window at the east end in memory of the sixth Earl of Carlisle, and one at the west end in memory of the Rev. Chas. Hardwick, born in Slingsby and baptised in Slingsby church, October 14th, 1821. An obituary notice of him will be found in the *Gentleman's Magazine* for 1859. He received from Mr Chapman, the village schoolmaster, the rudiments of knowledge, and passing rapidly through other schools, entered Catharine Hall, Cambridge, in 1841. He was a scholar by nature, and industrious as the bee, hiving up knowledge from every possible source. Self-help was the rule of his life. His books on "the Prayer Book," on "the Christian Church," and on "the thirty-nine articles of religion," are standard works, and the lectures which he delivered as Christian advocate of the University under the title of "Christ and other Masters," were one of the earliest attempts made in England towards the treatment of the science of comparative religions. He was no mere bookworm, but keenly interested in all philanthropic movements, specially in foreign mission work ; a zealous supporter of the universities' mission to Central Africa ; and one of the deputation from Cambridge that waited on the sister University of Oxford on this matter. His success in life did not lead him to forget the humble cottage of his birth where his father lived and worked as a joiner, for I have been told by many that he would often revisit Slingsby and express the delight which he felt in being once again in the old home.

Unfortunately his career was as brief as it was brilliant, for shortly after his appointment to the archdeaconry of Ely he perished at the early age of 37 from a fall in the Pyrenees, having ventured alone on a difficult mountain path. He is buried in the Protestant cemetery of Lachon. The window to his memory shows the figures of St Augustine, the Venerable Bede and St Jerome, with scenes from the lives of each in the lower lights; three men selected, no doubt, because of their literary labours in connection with the Holy Scriptures, and their consequent fitness to be associated with one who, though born in poor circumstances, did by dint of his patient labour, combined with his excellent gifts, win for himself a high place among ecclesiastical authors.

Charles Hardwick had as a friend and school-fellow John Close. The latter was born in Sinnington, but was brought to Slingsby in his early youth, where he attended Slingsby school. The story is that one day the two friends set out to make their way in the world and parted on Whitwell Hill, Charles Hardwick saying to his friend by way of pleasantry,

"When next we meet you will be a Lord Mayor, and I will be a bishop." The former portion of the prophecy was amply fulfilled, for John Close had a distinguished career, and was made three times Lord Mayor of York. He always attributed his success in life to the principles inculcated in him by Bridget Spenceley, with whom he was brought up when in Slingsby. She is now commemorated by a little oval window in the Wyville chapel; two other windows illustrating "Justice" and "Charity" and the text, "Her children shall rise up and call her blessed," commemorate John Close and his wife. All three have been erected by their sons, Henry and Charles. There are two other stained glass windows, one in the south wall of the sanctuary to the memory of the Rev. W. Walker, the other in the north wall of the nave to the memory of George Young, for fourteen years churchwarden. There is also a mural tablet by Salviati of marble and mosaic to the memory of Dr Lascelles and his wife.

Dr Lascelles was for forty-five years physician in Slingsby, and was universally respected and loved.

There are three bells in the tower : all three inscribed thus : " Dalton fecit. 1803," the largest, which is in connection with the clock and strikes the hours, has in addition the following, $\frac{\text{" M. Boyes,}}{\text{" T. Dobson,}}$ church-wardens." The church plate consists of a large pewter flagon, a silver paten, presented by the Hon. and Rev. E. T. Howard, rector in the year 1832 ; and a very elegant silver chalice. J. M. Fallow, an authority in antiquities, to whom I sent tracings of the markings on the chalice, wrote in reply : " Your chalice is of some interest. The ornamental border is very unusual. I have never met with one like it before. The marks are clearly old York. They are half leopard head and half fleur de lys, York town mark. Capital old English ' I,' the York ' date letter ' for 1616-17, which agrees nicely with the inscribed date ; the maker's mark, P. P.,

Peter Pearson of York, Goldsmith, free of that city in 1603. He made a communion cup and cover at Holy Trinity, Goodram-gate, York, and also repaired the Maize Bowl at York Minster."

A further addition was made to the altar-plate in the gift by Mrs Slater of a handsome brass alms-dish with the following inscription : " To the glory of God, and in loving memory of Elijah Slater, J.P., who died at Slingsby Hall on the 12th day of December in the year of our Lord 1399."

The registers begin in 1687, the first entry being " George, son of Richard Thompson, baptized May 24, 1687." The following year, 1688, the year of the Revolution, is a blank; and again there is a gap of eight years between August 1728 and July 1736. About eight leaves have been cut out of the inside of the next register, comprising entries from 1736 to 1721. Mr Walker mentions a report which may account for this mutilation of church property. He

says : " A certain over-indulgent clerk
sustains the reputation of having given
the parchment leaves of which several of
the registers were composed to various
industrious seamstresses to convert into
thread-holders." Although it is no pallia-
tion of the offence, it is fair to add that
the leaves cut out were probably blank,
for spaces exist in the first register for the
missing entries. The keepers of our
registers seem to have been of a con-
servative turn of mind, for they continued
to place baptisms, marriages, burials all
together under one heading from Lady
Day to Lady Day, even after the change
in 1752 from the old to the new style ;
nor was the new style adopted until 1812,
when under the act of Sir Geo. Rose,
printed register books were for the first
time brought into use. There is little else
to record with respect to our registers.
They contain no mention of "burials in
wollen": what they chiefly witness to is the
longevity of the population, for I find that
out of the 606 burials which took place dur-

ing the fifty years between 1834 and 1884,
seventy-two were persons eighty years old
and upwards, and of these four were
ninety years of age, two were ninety-one,
one was ninety-six, and one was ninety-
eight.

At the close of this chapter will be
found a list of the rectors. Samson, the
first on the list, was secular clerk when
Robert Chambord conferred the church
on Whitby Abbey, and according to the
terms of the gift was retained in his position. Michael, the second on the list,
was living in 1202, for in that year thére
was an exchange of tofts between him and
William de Eton and Pania his wife
(Pedes finium). Edmunde de Hawkesgarth was living in 1339, for in that year
he and William de Hawkesgarth acknowledge that they owe to Walter de Crayk
Knt 20 marks, to be levied in default of
payment on their lands and chattels, and
Edmunde's ecclesiastical goods (Pat. Rol.;
13 Ed. III., p. i, m. 49).

Torre gives the following notice of

testamentary burials, showing that six at least of the rectors were buried in the old church.

TESTAMENTARY BURIALS

A.D. 1390

Thomas Rykeley, 1391.—Thomas Rykeley Rector of the Church of Slingsby made his will proved 9 Oct. 1391, giving his soul as above and his body to be buried in the Church of All Saints' of Slingsby.

28 MARCH, A.D. 1419

William Gybson, 1419.—William Gybson Rector of the Parish Church of Slingsby in Rydale made his will, proved 6 April 1419 giving his soul to Almighty God, St Mary, and All Saints and his body to be buried in the Chancel of the Church of Slingsby.

8 JULY, 1443.

John Gare, 1443.—John Gare Rector of the Church of Slingsby made his will proved 14 Oct. 1449, giving his soul as above and his body to be buried at the entrance of the Quire at the south end of the high altar.

27 JULY, 1509.

John Fons, 1509.—John Fons Rector of the Parish Church of Slingsby, made his will proved Aug. 1509, giving his soul as above and his body to be buried at the entrance of the Quire of the Parish Church of Slingsby.

14 MARCH, A.D. 1522.

William Nicholson, 1526. — William Nicholson parson of Slengesbi made his will, proved 1 Feb. 1526 giving his soul as above and his body to be buried within the Choir of the Parish Church of All Hallows of Slengesbi.

24 JULY, 1592.

William Byrnand, 1592.—William Byrnand the late Parson of Slingsby made his will proved 5 Oct. 1592 giving his soul to God Almighty his Creator and Redeemer and his body to be buried in the Church of Slingesbye under the stone where Parson Nicholson was layd.

Some additional particulars with respect to the above John Fons are to be found in his will, dated 28th July 1509 ("York Wills Register," vol. viii. p. 16).

"He leaves to the heremite de Wath 1111^d, to the heremite de Gaunthorpe 11^d, to the heremite de Brandesley 11^d, also he wishes his executors to buy a white stone for xvi^s for his sepulchre."

When I came into residence I found in the rectory an old brass, which I have now framed and hung on the south wall of the church. It bears just sufficient traces of the lettering upon it to show that it is the brass referred to by Dodsworth with an inscription requesting prayers for the soul of one of the parsons of Slingsby, chaplain to the fourth Earl of Northumberland (see Ap. D). Eastmead, in his " Rievallensis," referring to this brass, gives the name of the parson as *Sir John Stone*, and the date 1608. This was very perplexing, for I could find no rector so named, either in Torres' MSS. or the archbishop's books. Accordingly I applied to the Bodleian for a copy of Dodsworth's notes, and in the one I received the name of the parson was thus written: " Sir John 'Hone," the note of interrogation over the " H " showing that the transcriber was uncertain as to the letter, and the date was not 1608 but 1508. Now, as 1509 is the date of the proving of John Fons' will, the date 1508 fits in nicely for the date of his death. Moreover, the brass in the old church lay just beneath the chancel step in the exact position in

which John Fons willed his body to be
buried. The conclusion was therefore
irresistible. The brass is in memory of
" John Fons." There was no such rector
as John Stone at all. Henry Percy,
fourth Earl of Northumberland, whom
John Fons served as chaplain, fell a
victim to the avarice of Henry VII. in
the year 1489. The Earl, being lieutenant
of the county, was called upon to collect
the subsidy granted to the king for the
war in Bretagne. The tax was exceedingly
unpopular, and the Earl wrote to the king
praying for an abatement; but the king
replied that not a penny should be abated,
which message, being incautiously delivered by the Earl to the populace, they
conceived him to be the cause of their
grievance, and breaking into his house,
Cocklodge, near Topcliffe, murdered him
and some of his attendants. Skelton,
poet-laureate, has described with what
manly courage the Earl fought on this
occasion, though cruelly forsaken, through
falsehood and fear, by those who should

have stood by him. The mutilated body was embalmed and brought with great pomp and ceremony to Beverley, where it now lies in the Minster, in the Percy Chantry. William Nicholson, who succeeded John Fons, was the last direct appointment made by Whitby Abbey. About thirty years afterwards came the suppression of the monasteries; then the patronage of the church passed for some years to the assignees of the abbot and convent, and from them it returned into the hands of royalty. Queen Elizabeth, in the year 1591, appointed John Phillips; and King James, in the year 1618, Samuel Phillips. John Phillips became Bishop of Sodor and Man in 1605, respecting whom I received from the present Bishop of Carlisle, when he held the see of Sodor and Man, the following information taken from Bishop Vowler Short's MSS. in Bishopscourt:—

" Bishop Phillips was a native of North Wales, and received his academical education in Oxford, became afterwards parson

of Thorpe-Bassett, and Slingsby, in Yorkshire, which latter he obtained in the
latter end of March 1591. About that
time, he, being chaplain to Henry, Earl of
Derby, became Archdeacon of Cleveland
on the resignation of Richard Bird, B.D.,
in April 1601, also Archdeacon of the
Isle of Man, and at length (about 1605)[1]
bishop of that place. He was presented
some time after his consecration, by the
Earl of Derby to the rectory of Ha-
warden, in Flintshire. He died August
7, 1663, and was privately buried, perhaps at his own desire, in the Cathedral
of St Germain."

Bishop Phillips used to preach in the
Manx language, and is the author of the
oldest Manx text—being the Book of
Common Prayer, translated in the early
portion of the seventeenth century, and
published for the first time in 1893, under

[1] The date 1614, given in Wood's Ath., is incorrect,
as shown by the fact that there is in the Registry,
Bishopscourt, a paper beginning, "In capella Sancti
Petri in Holme Vicessimo die Maii 1610, convocatio
habita eodem die coram domino Episcopo Jo. Phillips."

the editorship of Mr A. W. Moore, editor of the " Manx Note-Book."   The reforms which he planned for his diocese were received with opposition and jealousy by the governor of the island, John Ireland, who told the bishop that, being a Welshman, he never could do any good : their first difference arose out of a point which proves the bishop to have been anxious to retain old customs.   It was usual for claims on the estate of a deceased person to be proved by the claimant making an oath, lying upon his back on the grave with a Bible in his hand, in the presence of the compurgators.   The governor was for abolishing the custom, but the bishop wished to retain it ; and it remained in vogue for some considerable time after this dispute.

John Phillips was succeeded by Samuel Phillips, and Samuel Phillips by Enoch Smickler.   The institution of Enoch Smickler is not recorded in the archbishop's books, but his name appears in an enclosure award dated 1655

("Castle Howard Papers"). His Christian name bespeaks the Puritan, and he was probably a nominee of the Parliament. Shortly after the Restoration, Henry Beach was appointed rector by the Duke of Newcastle (1662). He was followed by two of the name of Robert Ward, probably father and son, one instituted in 1668, the other in 1689. The latter was also rector of Stokesley, to which rectory he was instituted on Jan. 25, 1688. He left by a deed dated January 4, 1712, a rent charge of £5, granted out of the property of Ann Mann, in Stokesley, for the use of the schoolmaster in Slingsby for teaching ten poor children to read and write, to be named and appointed by the minister and churchwardens of the time being of the parish. He seems to have resigned the living of Slingsby in 1718; and as patron for that turn to have conferred it on his son-in-law Robert Fish. He continued, however, to hold the living of Stokesley till his death in Dec. 1723. I have in my possession a copy of his will, proved in 1726, in which he says : I leave to my two daughters, Mary Fish and Elizabeth Moore, all my household goods and furniture whatever in the parsonage house at Stokesley, to be equally divided betwixt them. Then I give to my son William Ward, Dr of Laws, and his wife, each of them, ten broad pieces of gold. Then I give £10 to the poor of Stokesley, £10 to the poor of Slingsby, and 40s. to the poor of Hovingham." The £5 rent charge on the property of Ann Mann is now regularly paid, and is part of the general funds of the school. Robert Fish was succeeded by James Garden. He was ordained in 1713, and must, therefore, have been at least eighty-three when he died. I learn from the registers that he was a widower in 1744, when he married Sarah Stainforth, daughter of John Stainforth, late Lord Mayor of York. She died in 1764, and her tombstone, which I found in the rectory orchard, I have placed in the churchyard, leaning against the tower. In this same year, Archbishop Drummond sent a paper of questions to the clergy of his diocese, and the following is a copy of the answers of the Rev. James Garden, given me by the late Rev. A. Wetherall, rector of Stonegrave and rural-dean.

"Answer 1. — There are 69 families in the parish, no dissenters, unless methodists may be termed such, who are much displeased to be ranked under that denomination, as they profess themselves members of the church, and do actually attend divine service all but one, a licensed preacher.

"Answer 2.—The methodists, however, have a licensed meeting House in the parish. Their meetings are uncertain, having no settled teacher, sometimes once a week, sometimes once a fortnight, as they have a teacher. About ten persons have joined their society, but some others occasionally go to their meetings. The licensed preacher above mentioned is sometimes their teacher.

"Answer 3.—There is settled on the schoolmaster a salary of £5 per annum for teaching ten poor children to read and write. It was left above 40 years since by the late Mr Robert Ward, rector of this parish, and he has charged an estate he purchased of Ann Mann, widow, deceased, with the payment of the money, in the parish of Stokesley, in Cleveland. The salary is punctually paid by his grandson, Robert Ward, Esq., of York.

"Answer 4.—A piece of land lying in this parish called the poors' Close, which is let at six pounds per annum, was left to the poor of this parish about 50 years since by one George Burnet, of Slingsby. Besides this, and Mr Ward's donation above mentioned, there is neither alms house, hospital, or any other charitable endowment, nor any lands left for the repair of the Church, or any other pious use whatever.

"Answer 5.—I do reside personally upon my cure, and in the parsonage house, and have resided in them ever since I came to Slingsby.

"Answer 6.—Though hitherto I have not had a Curate, yet, being now far advanced in years, I purpose to employ one for four or five months next winter, if it please God so long to continue my life, and during that time, by your grace's permission, to repair to York, as I now sensibly find the country air too sharp in that cold season.

"Answer 7.—I perform divine service nowhere but in my own church, always read prayers and preach every Sunday morning and on Christmas Day and Good Friday; never omitted evening prayer on the Lord's Day but two or three months in the last winter on account of the badness of the weather.

"Answer 8.—I know of no unbaptized person that comes to church. But I believe several come to church who never were confirmed. I have baptized no adults since your Grace was our Archbishop.

"Answer 9.—I have not been able of late, as formerly, to catechize the children on the wednesdays and fridays in Lent, and therefore have delegated this office to the schoolmaster, a religious, good man, who catechises his scholars twice a week all the year round in the church catechism.

"Answer 10. — The Sacrament of the Lord's Supper is administered four times in the year, viz., at Christmas, Easter, Whit-Sunday, and the Feast of St Michael. Notice is given the Sunday before the administration; the number of Communicants is about two hundred, of these between twenty and twenty-four usually receive the Eucharist, and thirty-three received at Easter last. I have never had reason to refuse the Sacrament to any person.

"Answer 11.—There is no chapel belonging to this parish.

"Answer 12.—No public penances have been performed since your Grace was our Archbishop, neither did I ever hear of any commutations for penance since I belonged to the Diocese.

"Slingsby, R., James Garden, M.A.
    Instituted March 12, 1739."

James Garden died in 1773, and was succeeded by the Rev. John Cleaver, first cousin to the Rev. William Cleaver, tutor to the Duke of Buckingham in 1768, and afterwards Bishop successively of Chester, Bangor, and St Asaph. When William Cleaver presided over the diocese of Bangor, a few words spoken to an old servant brought him into conflict with De Quincey, who has related the circumstances in his " Confessions of an Opium Eater," with all that wealth of detail of which he was so consummate a master, and in which he so delighted to expatiate.

John Cleaver died on August 5, 1823, and was buried at Holme Pierrepoint. His successor, the Hon. and Rev. Henry Howard, the tenth and last child of Frederick, fifth Earl of Carlisle, was born in 1795. He resigned the rectory of Slingsby for the deanery of Lichfield in 1833. For many years after he left, he used to be remembered at the rent-dinners at Castle Howard, the invariable order of the toasts being the Queen, Lord Carlisle, the Dean of Lichfield.

The Rev. William Walker was ordained deacon at St George's, Hanover Square,

on the 27th day of March 1820, and became curate of Slingsby under the Rev.
Dr Cleaver, on April 9th in the same year.
He served as curate also under the Hon.
and Rev. H. Howard, and then succeeded
him as rector in 1834.

It has been related to me that in his
days the Mormons visited Slingsby, preaching on the green, and being housed by one
Willie Brown. They are said to have
made some converts, but to have been
vehemently opposed by a certain individual called Caygill, who lodged with Mr
Smailes, tailor.

Mr Walker wrote a brief account of
Slingsby, which is now a rare pamphlet.
It was dedicated to "the Rt. Hon. Geo.,
6th Earl of Carlisle, K.G., by his Lordship's very grateful and humble servant,
W. Walker," and is described in the title-
page as "a slight compilation, being an
attempt to keep a little longer from oblivion
memorials locally interesting." I have had
occasion to make frequent mention of this
interesting little book. Among the re-

miniscences of Mr Walker's time that have been recalled for my benefit I may relate the following, though I must fail to reproduce the ludicrous way in which the story was told me by one now many years dead. It appears that in the days when a certain John Piercy was a youth, he had a jackdaw and a magpie that regularly attended church, though on different occasions. The jackdaw would meet the Sunday-school children on their way to church, and when the door was opened, dart in over their heads, and take up his position on a hat-rail nailed to the wall between two of the arches, provoking the whisper from those who sat beneath, " He's here again." Then as the service proceeded, with his head on one side, he would sometimes croak out something like a "What!" as though surprised at some observation that the preacher had made. The magpie generally chose to sit on the canopy over the pulpit, and from this coign of vantage would sometimes fly down and peck at the leaves of the clergyman's MS. This was very disconcerting to the congregation, and the preacher would sometimes be compelled to stop in his discourse until the intruder had been removed. St Francis himself, preaching to the birds, might have objected to such goings on; but Mr Walker, I have been told, was extremely partial to these birds, and when the wife of a farmer lately come to the parish urged him to take steps to keep them from entering the church, he is said to have replied, " Madam, how do you know that there will not be jackdaws and magpies in heaven ? "

Of the work and character of my predecessor, the Rev. William Carter, there is no need for me to speak. His memorial is written in language that those who run may read, in the lives and hearts of the people. I never had the privilege of seeing him, but often in my visitings have I come across traces of his religious influence. He was a man of a most kindly, genial, and sympathetic nature, with a strong sense of humour; a most cultured and attractive preacher of the evangelical type. Speaking of the rise of ritualism along the *street* villages, he is reported to have said that when he was gone the last interruption on the *Roman* road would be removed. He is commemorated by a brass on the north wall of the sanctuary.

Thirty-four rectors have succeeded one another in apparently uninterrupted sequence, with no break in the chain at the time of the Reformation. During all this period, 800 years at the least, there has been one spot of ground in the heart of the village where " the pure Word of God has been preached, and the sacraments duly administered according to Christ's ordinance," where those who, in the common phraseology of Yorkshire, have " got their time over," have been laid to rest in hope of a blessed resurrection. Dull, indeed, must be the man whom such thoughts move not to reverent emotion, and to the hope that England's ancient and sacred fanes may long remain as they have been in the past,

> " Consecrate to faith
> In Him who bled for man upon the cross,
> Hallow'd to revelation, and no less
> To reason's mandates, and the hope divine
> Of pure imagination—above all,
> To charity and love."
> W. WORDSWORTH.

CALENDAR OF THE RECTORS AND PATRONS OF SLINGSBY.

M = DEATH.   R = RESIGNATION.   .... = NOT KNOWN.

Date of Institution.	Rector's Name.	Patron.	Cause of Vacancy.	Authority.
12th Cent.	Samson (Secular Monk).	William Hai and Robert Chambord.	....	Whitby Cartulary.
Living in 1202. Feb. 16, 1303.	Michael. Peter de Scheringdon, Priest.	Abbot and Convent of Whitby.	....	Pedes Finium. Torre's MSS. and Abp.'s Institution Bks.
	William Dareyns, Priest.	,,	R. for Church of Walkington.	,,
Oct. 4, 1332.	John de Cornubia (formerly of Walkington).	,,	R. for Church at Kyrby.	,,
Nov. 10.	Edmund de Hawkesgarth. Richard de Welles.	,, ,,	R. for Church of St Sampson, York.	,, ,,
Oct. 12, 1350.	Robert de Hackthorp, formerly of St Sampson.	,,	R. for Church of St George, Fishergate, York.	,,
April 1, 1355.	Nicolas de Feriby (Clerk), formerly of St Geo. York.	,,	....	,,
Oct. 18, 1391.	Thomas Rykeley, Priest. William Gibson.	,, ,,	M. M.	,, ,,
April 7, 1419.	John Carleton, LL.D., Clerk.	,,	R.	,,
March 10, 1420.	William Harkness, Priest.	,,	R.	,,
Jan. 8, 1429.	John Gare, Priest.	,,	M.	,,
March 12, 1443.	Rob. Brown, instituted at Bishopthorpe.	,,	R. for Church of St Andrew of Wode Walton, Lincolnshire.	,,
Nov. 19, 1448.	Richard Knott.	,,	R.	,,
May 27, 1457.	Ralph Howyk, Priest.	,,	M.	,,
May 14, 1479.	John Founs, Priest.	,,	....	,,
Sept. 11, 1509.	William Nicholson.	,,	....	,,

Date	Name	Patron	Status	Authority
Jan. 30, 1526.	John Coltman.	Assignees of Abbot and Convent of Whitby, Brian Darley, Professor of Divinity, and George Evers, Public Notary for this turn.	M.	Torre's MSS., Abp.'s Bks., and Whitby Cartulary, No. 394.
May 6, 1553.	John Smith, Clerk.	Assignees of Abbot and Convent of Whitby.		Torre's MSS. and Abp.'s Bks.
March 4, 1591.	William Bernande, Clerk. John Phillips, Clerk, M.A.	Queen Elizabeth.	R.	" and MSS. at Bishops court, Isle of Man.
Jan. 12, 1618.	Samuel Phillips, Clerk.	King James.	R., Died Aug. 7, 1663, buried in the Cathedral of St Germain. M.	Torre's MSS. and Abp.'s Bks.
March 12, 1662. Aug. 29, 1668. 1689. 1718.	Enoch Smickler. living in 1655. Henry Beach, Clerk. Robert Ward, Clerk. Robert Ward, son of above. Robert Fyshe.	William Marquis of Newcastle. William Duke of Newcastle. Duke of Newcastle. Robert Ward, p.h.v.	R. R. M. 1739.	C. Howard Papers. Abp.'s Bks.
March 12, 1739.	James Garden, M.A.	Most Noble Katharine, Duchess of Buckingham and Normanby.	M. 1773.	Torre's MSS. and Abp.'s Bks., and Abp. Sharp MSS.
Feb. 25, 1773.	John Cleaver, M.A.	John Cleaver, of Carburton, in the County of Nottingham, p.h.v.	M. 1823.	"
Aug. 22, 1823. Collated at same time to Sutton in the Forest.	Hon. and Rev. Henry Howard, M.A.	Rt. Hon. Fredk., Earl of Carlisle. Knt. of the Most Hon. Order of the Garter.	R.	"
May 15, 1834.	Rev. William Walker, M.A.	Rt. Hon. George, 6th Earl of Carlisle.	M., Aug. 15, 1855.	"
Nov. 21, 1855.	Rev. William Carter, M.A.	Rt. Hon. George William Frederick Howard, 7th Earl of Carlisle.	M., June 3, 1882.	"
July 31, 1882.	Rev. Arthur St. Clair Brooke, M.A.	Trustees, Earl of Carlisle.		"

CHAPTER VII

SOME CHANGES AND SURVIVALS

FOREMOST among the changes in an agricultural village must be reckoned those dealing with the land. Much may be learned in this direction from the old field names. I have added to the map of Slingsby all the field names mentioned in the tithe map (1848), as well as those that I have come across in conversation with old inhabitants of the place. In treating of this subject it is necessary to remember that a great portion of the country was once covered with wood, and that any clearance of flat ground, such as might be used for common or tillage, was called by the Anglo-Saxons, a field, as by the Norwegians a thwaite. When any such clearance was divided up by hedges or fences,

so as to form fields in our modern ac-
ceptation of the word; very often the
old name survived and was given to all
the enclosures thus formed; hence when
we find many fields bearing one name
we may conclude that we have here
an old field name. A glance at our
map will furnish many examples of this;
thus south of the railway we find Millgates and Gallows Hill both common
to seven fields. Harrow Balk and
Lawns, both common to five fields.
Pot, common to three fields. Whilst
north of the railway we have the name
Low common to seven fields, Marlbro' common to five, Holmsyke to
four, Bean and Holegate each common
to three.

With respect to the origin of these
names, Millgates or Mellgate is probably derived from the windmill which
existed somewhere in this part. In the
return of the lay-subsidies, granted to
Edward I., we have the names of two
millers in Slingsby (Ap. B), and the

Inq. p.m. of John Wyville taken in the same year states that John de Wyvell at the time of his death had in Slingsby two water-mills under one roof and one windmill (see Chap. IV.). Mill-Holm fixes where the ancient water-mill must have stood, and in the neighbouring Damsfield may still be traced the banks that once confined the waters of the mill-race. There was another mill at Fryton, for we have in the Rievaulx Cartulary (No. 310) Hugo de Flammarille giving to the Church of St Mary Rievaulx his mill "de Fritona quod vocatur Poxato juxta Haiam de Slengesbi." This must have been before the time of Abbot Roger (*i.e.* before 1224-39), for in his reign the Abbot and Convent of Rievaulx let to the Prior and Convent of Newburgh this same mill at Fryton (see Charter No. 312).

The name Gallows Hill is explained by a Pleading Roll of 1293, in which William de Wyville claims to have thief jurisdiction and a gallows in Slingsby (see Chap. IV.). Harrow-Balk is written Harwood Balk in an old survey in Castle Howard Office, dated 1702 ; this suggests that Harwood was the tenant, and that the field was called after him Harwood's field by the balk. In confirmation of this there is an indenture, dated Sept. 1, 1627, of the sale of a messuage and eight oxgangs of land by Francis Harwood and his son to Sir Charles Cavendish, Knt. (C. H. Papers.) The Lawns and Park fields perpetuate the memory of the park which once surrounded the castle, the wall of which may still be traced, within which deer, hares, and rabbits were probably preserved for the use of the proprietor and his household; the affix Priests attached to one of the park fields is due to the fact that this field was, for a considerable time, in the possession of one of the rectors.

Professor L. Miall, writing on the natural history of Craven, observes that near Horton and Selside are many pits in the limestone known locally as "pots" (*e.g.* Thirl-pot, Thund-pot, Hellen-pot). This suggests that our pot fields are named after the disused limestone quarry or serpent's hole in Low-pot-field ; a more likely derivation than one once given me by an old man, who said they were called pot-fields, because the stones in them when struck together made a jingling sound. Ings is a well-known name for low-lying meadows, generally near a river. The name Low-fields is explained by the position of the land, which is not more than ninety-one feet above the sea-level. Marlbro' is written Mawbourne in old documents. I cannot account for the word. The Holm-syke fields are named after the syke or little trickling rivulet which runs here, separating the townships of Slingsby and South-Holm. The first syllable of Holegate is the old English howl or hollow, denoting low-land. When the children of Slingsby wish to play in the castle moat, they say, " Let us go and play in the howl." The second syllable is familiar in cowgate—*i.e.* cow-way or cow-pasture. Among names confined to single fields, we have eastward hills and westward hills. The absence of any rising ground in the neighbourhood of these fields, as well as their proximity to three closes called Mason, favours the view that the word "hills" here may stand for enclosure; and this observation may apply also to Car hills, south moor hills, and middle moor hills—all in the low country.[1]

Whatever doubts may be felt about this definition, dissociating the word "hills" from any idea of elevation, there can be no doubt that "dale" in Wandales has

[1] The Rev. M. Morris, writing in the "Transactions of the E. R. Antiquarian Society," vol. vi. p. 5, says, "It by no means follows that the use of the term *hill*, as applied to a field, indicates rising ground. I connect this with the dialectic word *hull*, which is commonly used to denote the outer shell or covering of peas, nuts, etc., being that which holds or encloses the kernel. It is somewhat remarkable that *hills*, meaning enclosed places, seem to be most frequently met with in the flattest parts of the Riding."

nothing to do with a depression of land such as we think of when we speak of hills and dales. The name prevails almost everywhere in the north. It is compounded of the Scandinavian "wang," a field, and "dale," a portion (cp. to deal as in cards), only there is a difference of opinion as to whether "wang" in Wandales means an open field or enclosed land. Totten Bridge is, I think, short for Town-end Bridge, being on Totten or Town-end Lane. In an old survey of the Slingsby estate taken in 1702, in the time of the Duchess of Buckingham, we find the following additional field names, but their exact position I have not been able to identify: "Greedy Flat," "Long Clack," "Bullwray," "Swim Potts," "Mighty Hill Lands," "Boodills," "Watticall," "Far Wandales" (C. H. Papers).

We have seen how, in Domesday time (chap. ii.), the land of the village lay in large open common fields, arable, meadow, and pasture, the villeins, or small farmers, having a share in each. The arable then, and for many years afterwards, was divided into acre or half-acre strips, separated from one another by turf balks. The villeins held, as a rule, a score or more of these strips, not lying side by side, as we should have supposed, but scattered here and there over the whole field in different directions. A third or half of the arable was always in fallow, and the intermixture of plots rendered necessary a fixed system of working the land. No one farmer could do what he liked with his strips. There was a rigid law, handed down from remote ages, which settled the times and the seasons for the various processes of sowing, reaping, etc.

It is easy to see how inconvenient this common-field system of agriculture must have been; how much time was wasted in cattle and labourers travelling to many dispersed pieces of land; how little encouragement a farmer had to do the best with his land. He might free his strips of weeds, but unless his neighbours did the same, his oxgangs would soon be sown with his neighbour's weeds. He might wish to drain his portion, but what chance had he of carrying off the water when somebody else's land would probably lie in the course of the fall? Moreover we are told that the land-marks defining each man's portion were often indefinite ; hence quarrels would often arise, and in spite of the injunction of Queen Elizabeth (1559), ordering the curate on Rogation days to admonish the people, saying, "Cursed be he that translateth the bonds and doles of his neighbour," dishonest farmers would plough at night and steal a furrow from their neighbour's strips or from the balks. It is strange that this old system lasted so long as it did ; but it was replaced at last by the modern system of enclosed fields separated from one another by hedges and ditches, and the farmer received in lieu of his scattered oxgangs a more or less compact block of the same extent, which he could do with as he liked. This

change, which altered the whole face of the
country and the position of the farmer by
doubling and trebling the value of the
land, was brought about very gradually—
sooner in one place than another. In
Slingsby one hundred years intervened
between the enclosure of one part of
the parish and another. Marshall, in his
"Rural Economy of Yorkshire," written
in 1796, points out that there were three
different methods of enclosure in the
Pickering Vale, *i.e.* (1) enclosure by
amicable exchanges and transfers; (2)
enclosure by private commission, when
the lands were laid out by commissioners
chosen unanimously by the several
interests concerned without soliciting the
assistance of Parliament; (3) enclosure
by Act of Parliament. The fields called
"hills" and "closes" may be an instance of the first of these methods.
We have an undoubted instance of the
second, when 354 acres north of Greendyke Lane were enclosed in 1655 by
private commission.

I give the opening words of the Award from a copy in the Estate Office of Castle Howard :—

" It was agreed by and betwixt the Rt. Hon. Charles Viscount Mansfield, Henry Cavendish his brother, and George Hill, Thos. Hutchinson, Robert Robson, William Sellers, Thos. Manson, Thos. Burnand, with the consent of and approbation of the Hon. Charles Howard, Esqre., as also by and with the consent of Enoch Smickler, the Minister and Rector of the Parsonage, and Church of Slingsby, that there should be a general enclosure and improvement of all lands, meadows, and commons lying, and being below the hill and abutting upon the furlongs called the New Dyke and Barton footway, and that every man's land may be estimated, valued, and plotted in such measure, that each man may have all advantage of lands together, according to the worth, quantity, and quality of the lands they hold together."

This was a very early enclosure for this

part of the country, for Marshall, writing at the close of the eighteenth
century, says of the Vale of Pickering:
" In my own remembrance more than
half the Vale lay open," but enclosures
once begun rapidly increased; and he
adds: " Now scarcely an open or undivided common remains."

As an instance of the third method of
enclosure, we have an Act passed in 1755
entitled, " An Act for dividing, and enclos-
ing several open fields, and pastures or
common in the township of Slingsby.
All the land dealt with was south of
Greendyke Lane, and the amount was
909 acres. The whole lay in the
common open fields in the following
measurements, *i.e.* in Harrow-Balk field,
229 acres, 2 roods, 18 poles; in Gallow
Hill field, 200 acres, 1 rood, 8 poles; in
Pott field, Melgate and Wandales, 239
acres, 1 rood, 24 poles ; in the common
called Slingsby Moor, 237 acres, 2 roods,
9 poles; in commonable ground in Greendyke Lane, 2 acres, 2 roods, 16 poles. The

parties to the enclosure were the Right Hon. Henry, Earl of Carlisle, who received as his share 701 acres, 2 roods, 33 poles; the Rev. James Garden, who received 42 acres, 1 rood, 24 poles in lieu of eight oxgangs of glebe and common rights; Robert Ward, who received 117 acres, 29 poles; and the following freeholders, amongst whom the rest of the land was divided, *i.e.* W. Peacock, Richard Nesse, Wm. Blackbeard, Nicolas Manners, Bartholomew Dobson, Francis Isherwood, George Hebden, Edward Hardesty, and Elizabeth Waite. The commissioners were Samuel Milbourn, Wm. Richardson, and John Conyers. The Rev. James Garden received as satisfaction for tithes on certain lands a modus or composition of £64. This settlement of a portion of the tithe for a fixed payment was followed in 1848 by a fixed rent charge of £369 for all the still uncommuted tithes. From that date all Slingsby tithes ceased to be paid in kind, but even earlier than this it had been customary to commute for a money payment, at least the smaller tithes, for in an old terrier, bearing date 1760, the tithing of calves, wool, and bees is made payable in money, although the tithing of corn was still paid in kind.

In my predecessor's days an old tithe barn stood in the rectory grounds, which was used for divine worship when the church was being rebuilt. It was afterwards taken down, and the material went to erect a shed in the yard of the glebe farm tenant. An old man, now dead, who served one of the rectors of Barton-le-Street, told me that it was his business to collect the tithe of corn, which he did by going to the harvest field and marking off each tenth stook with a green twig. When I asked him how the farmers liked this, he said, " There was a good deal of bad language, but this was only their contrariness ; it was the law, and they had to put up with it."

When the Malton and Thirsk branch of the N. E. Railway was being made, 2 roods and 35 perches of the glebe were sold, and the sum of £43, 6s. 4d. consolidated 3 per cent. stock purchased, which afterwards was exchanged for local loans of the same amount. This is now in the hands of the Ecclesiastical Commissioners, and yields to the benefice 25s. per annum. Mr Walker turned six acres of the glebe in Harrow-Balk fields into allotments, which used to be let out in half-rood portions with the object of encouraging spade-culture ; but the decrease in the population, and the increased facilities for acquiring allotments which now exist, have resulted in reducing the number of occupants from twenty-four to twelve.

With the changes in the land of the parish due to enclosures may be associated those later changes due to the introduction of machinery. There are old folks in Slingsby who wax eloquent describing the time when the whole village turned out to gather in the harvest—women and children as well as men and boys—and when the farmers gave their mell suppers (*i.e.* meal, or perhaps mingling supper, where rank and status were laid aside). I have been specially informed how fine a sight it used to be to see, on a bright day, eleven or twelve men mowing the meadows of Castle Howard, all swinging together at their work to the tune of their scythes. It seems that the mowers formed a complete society among themselves, and that they all had nicknames given them at a kind of baptism. The man to be named was held up in the arms of one of his fellows, whilst the "lord," or chief mower, cast a horn of beer over him and named him. In addition to the "lord" there was the "lady," who held rank after him ; and if any woman entered the field while the work was going on, it was the right of the lady to demand that she should pay her way by a kiss. The lord was chosen for his skill with the scythe, and, like the stroke-oar in a boat race, used to set the pace, which all the rest had to keep up with. There was a recognised code of manners in the society, and any one offending against the same had to submit to corporal punishment, which was administered with much judicial formality. The mowers worked by the piece, being paid so much per acre, consequently they were more or less their own masters. Sometimes, when they had a long distance to go, they would start as early as two o'clock in the morning, but they made up for this by taking considerable intervals of rest during the day, three hours for dinner and other off-times for other meals not being unusual. There is an old man, hale and hearty, still living in Slingsby, one of the few survivors of these old times. He has given me the following as the nicknames by which he and his fellow-mowers were known, *i.e.* Dumpleby, Tiger, Swift, Spotty, Buffalo, Gaping Geese, Rover, Bummle-Kite (blackberry).

In connection with the changes in agriculture may be mentioned some that have taken place in the social life of the place. Mr Walker tells in his history how, in his days, the pillion on which the village matron used to be carried to market had disappeared, also the stocks, long after it had fallen into disuse. Wordsworth, in one of his sonnets, laments the loss of the spinning-wheel in the Lake Country.

"Grief, thou hast lost an ever present friend
Now that the cottage wheel is mute."

The spinning-wheel was a familiar adjunct of cottage life in Slingsby in the old days. There were many who "swiftly turned the murmuring wheel"; but even more popular was the handloom. In Mill-Holm there used to be two ponds, one of which was called Line-pond, where the flax was steeped and prepared for weaving purposes; and in some of the houses sheets still exist that were woven in the village. A reference to the registers shows that many followed this occupation. Thus we have " Elizabeth, wife of Isaac Campleman, weaver, buried Jan. 22, 1753;" "William Boyes, weaver, buried July 2nd, 1780;" " Christopher Hesp, weaver, buried June 1782;" "William Skelton, weaver, buried 1801;" "Wm. Dale, weaver, buried 1805;" " The children of Wm. Dawson, weaver, baptised 1800 and 1802;" "Anne, daughter of John Horner, weaver, baptised 1809." Mr Walker in his history thus refers to this trade: "In the recollection of the writer of this compilation there were two or three hand-looms here in full employment for weaving linen: improvements in machinery have stopped them. All the weavers but one have quitted this earthly scene, and he is a spare old man stooping under the weight of years—John Horner, the last of the weavers." The said John Horner was buried by Mr Walker, Jan. 26, 1852, aged seventy-four years. With John Horner, the last of the weavers, may be compared Henry, the first in the trade whose name has come down to us, and who was living in 1300 (see Ap. B). Candle-making was another trade now extinct. It lasted on to a later period than weaving, and many of the present generation remember it well.

Among the sports and pastimes that have died out, may be reckoned Plough Monday processions (the Monday next after twelfth day). These were common in the early part of the last century. I have heard that great rivalry existed between Terrington and Slingsby in these performances. Terrington would parade with garland dancers, and Slingsby with sword-dancers, then the spokesman of the Slingsby company having formed a ring, would step into the middle and address the Terrington company in the following doggerel rhyme :—

"Garlands make room, I pray, for here you plainly see
Six youths in pink and blue, who now do follow me.
They'll do the best they can, so let them try their skill.
Music, strike up and play "t' auld wife o' Coverdale."

Again, there was the "Free Hunt" which was held on November 5th. The morning was ushered in by a peal from the church bells. Dogs came from all parts. Coursing was allowed all over the Carlisle estate. Multitudes of hares and rabbits were killed ; and afterwards cooked and distributed gratis among the villagers. Another sport that now only exists in the remembrance of those who once enjoyed it, was Knutspell, locally called Dab Spell, a game played now a great deal in the West Riding and referred to by Strutt in his "Sports and Pastimes," under the title of "Northern Spell." Thirty years ago it was a great favourite here. It was played on the flats, and Shrove Tuesday was a special day for it. On the previous Monday, "Collop Monday," the boys of the school were accustomed to have a barring-out. They locked the door and crept under the forms, and when Mr Chapman, who was schoolmaster at this time, came round, he found a notice on the school door in doggerel rhyme dispensing with his services for the afternoon. Jove himself has been known to nod, and Mr Chapman, it is said, generally accepted the situation with a good grace, and went home, pleased it may be to have a temporary rest from work and the exercise of discipline. From all accounts he was an "awfu' severe man." He had hazel

twigs brought to him by one of his pupils
who lived in the wood, which were hung
up as a terror to evil doers, and a ruler
which he cast with unerring aim at the
head of any offending boy, who was compelled to return it, knowing that he was
about to receive a further taste of its
quality. Sunday and day school were
then in partnership, and a mistake in the
repetition of the collect on Sunday meant
the stick on Monday, and as there were
some who never could learn the collect,
their Sundays were overshadowed by
somewhat gloomy forebodings. Barring-
out ceased in Mr Germain's time, Mr
Chapman's successor. I have heard a
great deal of the hardships of school in
his days: the cold of the room, the additional charge made for coals and ink,
the high fees. All this has now changed.
Education is free, corporal punishment
the exception rather than the rule. The
Slingsby people voted for a School Board,
and one was formed for the united districts
of Slingsby, Fryton, and South-Holm on

October 1900, and now the school, in accordance with the Education Act of 1902, is under the authority of the North Riding County Council.

Before leaving the subject of change it may not be uninteresting to give the population of Slingsby during the last hundred years. The subjoined table from the Parliamentary returns shows how the population rose gradually from 434 in 1801, to 707 in 1861, since which time it has gradually decreased.

POPULATION OF SLINGSBY FROM 1801-1901.

Years.	Males.	Females.	Total.
1801	203	231	434
1811	227	237	464
1821	274	274	548
1831	279	283	562
1841	309	300	609
1851	307	325	632
1861	344	363	707
1871	311	337	648
1881	297	299	596
1891	253	273	526
1901	226	228	454

As in dealing with changes we began with those that had to do with the land, so in the matter of survivals we may mention that we have a relic of the old time when lands were held in common in the Priest's Park, which is now let out as a common pasture for a certain number of tenants, under the control of a pasture-master elected by themselves, as also in the Bean Land, a portion of which is still, what the whole used to be, common meadow, shared by different tenants, whose portions were marked off by stakes placed in the ground, the cattle ranging over the whole after the hay crop had been gathered in. We are reminded of another survival in connection with land as often as we see a notice which appears from time to time posted up in the church porch summoning to the court - baron and court-leet of the manor of Slingsby "the freeholders, tenants, and resiants to attend at the usual place and perform their suit and service, due and of right accustomed, on pain of being presented and fined for neglect or default." These courts used to manage the affairs of the manor, the court-baron having civil and the court-leet, which required a jury, criminal jurisdiction. Mr Walker states that the usual place of meeting was the south-east turret of the castle yard, though quite destroyed in his day. The courts exist now only in name, the business done being of a trifling description, such as the selection of a jury to see to the cleansing of the banks and ditches; but not long ago the bellman was appointed, and the pinder to pound wandering beasts, and surrenders and grants of tenancy were recorded.

Passing from the land we have an interesting survival in the Slingsby Maypole, 83 feet high, visible from a considerable distance, and giving the village a certain antique appearance. As Maypoles date back to very early days, having their origin in the welcome which from remote ages all nations have given to the coming of spring, it may be that when

Eslinc made Slingsby he put up a May-
pole. Here the freemen may have met
in the Danish "thring," which answered
to the English "moot," for Brand, quoting
from an old writer, says: "The column
of May was the great standard of justice:
here it was that the people, if they saw
cause, deposed or punished their governors,
their barons, or kings." Later on, when,
subsequent to the Norman Conquest,
Slingsby was held by Lord Hastings,
who had licence to enclose 2000 acres,
he may have given trees from his park,
to make the Slingsby column, as has
been the custom of the Earls of Carlisle since the village came into their
possession. The early Reformers looked
askance at Maypoles, and counted the
dances around them as an abomination;
and in the reign of Edward VI. the
Lords and Commons ordained "that all
and singular Maypoles that are, and shall
be erected, shall be taken down," at which
time the Slingsby pole, if such existed,
must have been removed with the rest;

but only for a time, for in 1633 King
Charles I. enacted "that for his good
people's lawful recreation they were not
to be disturbed or discouraged from
having May games, Whitsun ales, and
merry dances, and the setting up of
Maypoles," at which time we may take
it for granted the Slingsby Maypole
would flourish, for the place was in
the hands of the loyal Duke of Newcastle, who, in his devotion to his royal
master, would naturally see that all
his directions were faithfully carried out.
Upon the death of Charles I. the Long
Parliament waged war against Maypoles
as being associated with much drunken-
ness and licentiousness, and an order was
made for all Maypoles to be taken down,
and a fine of 5s. levied weekly on the
parish officer in whose parish a May-
pole was found still standing : but with
the Restoration (1661) there came another
change, and Maypoles were again erected
all over the country. The majority of
these have now disappeared, but York-

shire boasts of at least ten, amongst which
there are few, as far as I know, in such
good condition as that which now stands, a
column worthy of the admiration of all, on
the village green of Slingsby. Some
years ago I asked some of the old folks
how far back they could remember a May-
pole in Slingsby, and one old man told me
he remembered one being set up in 1814
and another in 1828 and another in 1864.
In consequence of some sap having been
left in the upper portion of the 1864 pole, it
had to be replaced by a new pole in 1871,
which stood 81 feet from the ground.
This was taken down for re-decoration
and repainting in 1880, and again in
the year of Victoria's Jubilee, 1887, on a
day that I remember well, for there was
a violent storm of hail phenomenal for
the time of year. It was under very
different circumstances that the present
pole was reared in 1895. The air
was warm, the sun shone bright, the
school was gay with flags ; with the help
of ropes and a crane, and a number of

willing hands the pole was slowly raised,
and when at last it stood straight up, and
the sun shone upon the three colours with
which it had been painted, the enthusiasm
broke out in cheers which were repeated
again and again when a daring spirit,
one of our most promising young men—
alas! now dead — climbed to the top
and turned round the gilded weather-
cock forming the vane.   The new tree to
form this pole was given from the Castle
Howard wood by Lord and Lady Carlisle.
It was drawn by hand from the top of the
sheep walk to the entrance of the village,
where the oldest man, one Tom Spenceley,
was placed sitting upon it; a procession
was then formed, which went round
the village, and ended by leaving the
tree on the green, where it was taken in
hand by joiners and decorators and soon
made ready for the day of erection, May
14th, when again a procession was formed,
the old custom being observed of calling
at the different houses for cheese-cakes
and spice-bread and other dainties for the

"rearing tea." This was duly given to the school children after they had plaited a miniature pole put up close at hand to the music of the Kirby-Moorside brass band. Thus began the Slingsby May-pole dances, which are now held nearly every year on the two feast days, May 13th and 14th, and witnessed by many from far and near.

Under the head of survivals may be placed some of our old institutions, old customs, and superstitions.

Among the old institutions of the place may be counted the Temperance Society, which was started as early as 1850, when an agent from Malton attended and addressed a small meeting in the yard at the back of the house of one Robert Smailes (tailor). The pledge taken was as follows : " We agree to abstain from all intoxicating liquors as beverages, and in all suitable ways to discountenance their use throughout the community." Among the first to sign were Robert Smailes, Thos. Britton, W. Witson, and J. Ezard. This was the

beginning of the Slingsby Total Absti-
nence Society, which has gone on with
varying success ever since.   As the
foundation of the English Temperance
Movement was not laid till July 1831,
when Joseph Livesey wrote in the *Moral
Reformer*, "While drinking continues
poverty and vice will prevail, and until
this is abandoned, no regulations, no
efforts, no authority under heaven can
raise the condition of the working classes,"
Slingsby may be considered as well in the
van in the battle against intemperance.
The early advocates of the movement, I
have been told, were violently opposed,
particularly by one individual, who made
it his business to attend the meetings with
the object of breaking them up ; but the
stalwart water-drinkers were a match for
him, and used to carry him away bodily
in their arms.   The Temperance ship sails
now in calmer waters, and the Slingsby
society has the firm support of Lord and
Lady Carlisle, who are both total ab-
stainers and ardent workers in the cause.

With respect to old customs, most weddings in Slingsby are terminated by the bride offering a ribbon to be run for by the youth of the village, no doubt a relic of the time when the bride was captured by the strongest and the fleetest. The waits go round on Christmas Eve singing at the different houses; one of their number finishes by calling out in a loud voice, "Good morning, Mr and Mrs —— (here the heads of the family are named), likewise all your family and your faithful servants"; then the hour of the morning and the state of the weather are loudly sung out.

With respect to superstitions it is considered unlucky for a young woman to attend church when her banns are published. It is thought that death-struggles are unduly prolonged by the presence of pigeons' feathers in the bed. I knew an old man who, at his own request, was taken off the bed and laid on the floor because it was thought that these ill-omened feathers were in his bed and prevented his passing away. I have also heard of an old doctor who, when any one was lingering long in his last sufferings, would always say with reference to this idea, " Is the bed right?"

It is regarded as very unlucky for the tenant of a house to be the first to enter it on New Year's Day. If he go out early he must get some boy or girl to come home with him, and to go in before him ; failing this he must get a sprig of green and throw it in, in front of him : thereby he disarms the evil influence ; and the boy or girl in question is called his "lucky" boy or "lucky" girl, and it is usual to present such with a cake or present of some kind.

These and such like superstitions are now fast passing away with the spread of education and the widening of knowledge, due in great measure to the ease and rapidity of modern travel. The bicycle has worked wonders in the habits of the present generation, enabling them to see places and things which the former generation, who were for the most part dwellers at home and among their own people,

never dreamt of visiting ; but if I mistake
not, these opportunities of roving have
not diminished aught of the peculiar
attachment which Slingsby people, in
common with all Yorkshire folk, have for
their native village. It seems as if I had
been inoculated with this sentiment on my
first coming, now twenty years ago; I
remember the day as though it were
yesterday, and the pleasant greeting which
the murmuring brook which flows hard by
the station gave me as I stepped from the
train : the same that greeted Dodsworth
on his visit now nigh 300 years ago,
and made him enter in his note-book,
" Slingsby is watered by a sweet rivulet " ;
nor have the after years belied these early
anticipations, but rather more than fulfilled them, for the place has grown dearer
to me with the flight of time, and with the
pleasure which I have felt in trying to
link its history to history in general. I say
nothing here of the friendships I have
made, nor of the many whom I have seen
depart in peace to brighter worlds, whose

memory will not fade. Enough if anything contained in this little book should make their home-land dearer to those who live here, or serve as an inducement to some chance reader to visit the place.

APPENDIX A

SLINGSBY IN KIRKBY'S INQUEST

1284-85

IN the thirteenth year of Edward I. a survey was
made of several of the counties of England by
the King's Treasurer, John de Kirkby, who, under
the authority of a Royal Commission, inquired,
according to the ancient custom by "inquests" or
"verdicts of juries," concerning all the immediate
tenants of the Crown. The purpose of the survey
was probably to afford the King more ample information than he previously possessed preparatory to the
issuing of writs of military service and the levying
of subsidies. It would be analogous to that valuation
of property which precedes the rating of the present
day. I give the portion of the inquisition relating to
Slingsby: " In Slingsby there are fifteen carucates
of land of the fee of Mowbray: out of which the
Church is endowed with one carucate tax free; and
the Templar Brothers hold two bovates tax free; and
the Canons of Kirkham two bovates of land tax free;
and the Canons of Malton one carucate tax free; and
John Chaumbard holds five carucates of the heirs of
Wake, and the heirs of Wake of Roger Mowbray, and

Roger Mowbray of the King in chief; and William de Wyvyll holds seven carucates of land and a half, taxable, of Roger Mowbray, and Roger Mowbray in chief of the King.   Seven carucates of land of the fee of Chaumbard make a Knight's fee; and twelve carucates of land of William de Wyvyll make a fee—makes an annual payment for the use of the wapentake of 10s. 4d."   The whole works out as follows:—

	Car.	Bov.
Church	1	0
Templars	0	2
Canons of Kirkham . .	0	2
Canons of Malton . . .	1	0
John Chaumbard . . .	5	0
William de Wyvyll . . .	7	4
	15	0

APPENDIX B

Yorkshire Lay Subsidies

The Parliament held in the spring of 1300-1, granted a subsidy of a 15th of all personality to Edward I. to help him in carrying on the Scotch campaign.   Goods held in a purely spiritual capacity were not to be taxed, but all temporal goods, whether belonging to ecclesiastics or laymen, or any person whatsoever in the realm, of whatever condition they were, might be taxed. The 15th was more widely levied than the 9th, granted in 1297. No return for the latter tax remains for the North Riding, but the returns for the 15th are, with some few exceptions, quite perfect. Very poor persons were taxed as well as the rich, for as small a sum as 2d. is not an uncommon entry. The Yorkshire returns only give the sum total, and do not specify the goods on which the 15th was levied, but some extracts from the returns of Colchester show what sort of goods were taxed and what their value was: thus we have "napkin and towel, 10d.;" "cow, 5s.; sow, 15d.; bed, 3s.; 2 towels, 12d.; 4 quarters of wheat, 12s., at 3s. per quarter; 60 sheep, 12d. each."

The return for Slingsby, which is given below, is very interesting, as it contains not only the names of the residents, but also some of the occupations or trades in vogue at the time. Thus we see that the two chief persons in the place (because they paid the highest tax) were William and Thomas Wyvile, each paying 10s.; then there was the Prior of Malton paying 4s. 10d., and the Parson paying 10d.; two Preceptors, or Bailiffs, Galdrifus, or Geoffrey, and John, one paying 3s. 6d., the other 2s. 1d. These probably kept the accounts of the two manors. In addition there were two Molendinarii, or Millers; one probably kept the windmill which has left its name in Mellgate, and the other the watermill which once stood near the station. Then there was William the Faber, or "Smith," and Henry the Tixtor, or Textor, that is "the Weaver." Every village would have its weaver. William the Triturator, *i.e.* the Thresher, one who used the flail; Gervais the "Falcator," the mower of grass; and John the Bubulcus, *i.e.* the keeper of the parish bull (Bubulcus), and hence probably the looker after cattle on the common fields. The word is a very exceptional one, and might safely be rendered oxherd, or cowherd, or herdsman, as opposed to shepherd.

YORKSHIRE LAY SUBSIDIES

SLENGESBY

De Willelmo de Wyvill	.	xs. ijd. oq.
De Priore de Malton	.	iiiis. xd.
De Persona de Slengesby	.	xd. o.
De Thoma de Wyvill	.	xs.
De Willelmo Molendinario	.	iis. viiid. o.
De Henrico Nodde	.	iis. viid.
De Isabella Fraunceys	.	iis. viid.
De Alano Milifray	.	xviiid.
De Johanne de Stodelay	.	iiis. vid.
De Galfrido Preposito	.	iiis. vid.
De Galfrido Molendinario	.	iis. id.
De Johanne Preposito	.	iis. id.
De Willelmo Fabro	.	iiis.
De Alicia Amyas	.	vis. viiid.
De Hugone Rol	.	xvid.
De Johanne de Cramevill	.	xviid.
De Radulpho de Barton	.	iiis. id.
De Galfrido Crameville	.	xiiid.
De Henrico Tixtore	.	xixd.
De Willelmo Trituratore	.	vid.

De Gervasio Falcatore   .   .   xiiid.
De Johanne Bubulco   .   .   iid.
De Alano Menur   .   .   .   iid.

APPENDIX C

The earliest and simplest way of transferring land
or property was by grant or charter. Very many of
these charters are now extant, preserved in various
places. Thus the church of Slingsby was conveyed
to Whitby Abbey by Wm. Hai and John Chambord
in the eleventh century, and the charter is now among
the deeds of the Abbey. Another way for the con-
veyancing of land is mentioned by Shakespeare in
"Hamlet," Act v., Sc. 1. Hamlet and Horatio are in
the graveyard. Hamlet takes up a skull thrown up by
the spade of the grave-digger and says, "This fellow
might be in's time a great buyer of land with his
statutes, his recognizances, his fines." The fine here
referred to is so called because it was the *final*
agreement or concord between two parties concerning
lands or rents or other matters. When two parties
had agreed to treat about the transfer of a piece of
land, etc., the person to whom the property was to
be conveyed, called the "Plaintiff," commenced a
suit of law against the owner or tenant, called "the
Deforciant." This was succeeded by an agreement
or concord putting *an end* (finis) to the suit in the
King's Court, which agreement was enrolled in the
records of the Courts, where it could at any time be

consulted by either party. The most important part of this document was the "foot of the fine," which always began thus: "Haec est finalis concordia facta," etc. It was a recapitulation of the whole matter, giving the name of the parties concerned, with the place and time of the transaction. "The feet of fines" were so called, not because they were at the foot of the documents, but by misinterpretation of the Norman French, "La pees"—modern French, "La paix," as though "pied"—foot. The "foot of the fine" was "the peace," the "final concord" between the litigants. These records form a series of documents which cover an unbroken period of six centuries from the time of Henry II. until the reign of William IV., when this mode of conveying land was abolished and more simple methods of assurance substituted.

The Yorkshire Archæological Society has published "the Yorkshire fines" for the Tudor period, from which I extract the following having reference to Slingsby :—

YORKSHIRE FINES

..	PLAINTIFF.	DEFORCIANT.	NATURE AND SITUATION OF PROPERTY.
1549-1550. Hilary Term, 3 Ed. VI.	John Yorke, Kt.	Francis, Earl of Huntingdon and Katherine his wife.	Manor of Slyngesby and 30 messuages with lands, and in Colton Holte Crofte, also advowson of Slyngesby Church.

YORKSHIRE FINES—*continued*

..	PLAINTIFF	DEFORCIANT.	NATURE AND SITUATION OF PROPERTY.
1562. Easter Term, 4 Elizabeth.	Raudus Harwar and Richard Whyt.	Henry, Earl of Huntingdon, and John Dawson, Gent.	Castle called Slyngesby Castle and 2 messuages with lands in Slyngesby, Cowton, Holdthorpe, and Hovyngham.
1563. Trinity Term, 5 Elizabeth.	John Atherton, Kt.	Henry, Earl of Huntingdon, and Katherine his wife, and Thomas Gerard, Kt., and Elizabeth his wife.	Manor of Slyngesby and 40 messuages and 10 cottages with lands in the same.
1564. Trinity Term, 6 Elizabeth.	Thomas Dacre, Kt., Lord Dacre of Gyllesland and Graistock, and Elizabeth his wife.	Wm. Carus, Serjeant, at law to the Queen, and Wm. Boswell, Queen's Solicitor.	Barony and Castle of Hyderskelf, also Hylderskelf with Manor of Slyngesby, Terrington, Woganthorpe, Ganthorpe, Amotherby, Thorpe Bassett, Holme, Etton, Birdsale, etc., etc., etc.
1585. Trinity Term, 27 Elizabeth.	James Tynessley, Gent.	John Atherton, Esq., and Katherine his wife, and Richard Atherton, Gent.	Manor of Slyngesby and 40 messuages, 40 cottages, and 2 water-mills with lands there and in Hovingham and Fryton.
1586. Hilary Term, 29 Elizabeth.	Thomas Ld. Howard, Henry Ld. Barkeley, Henry Knevett, Kt., Thomas Knevett, Esq., Thomas Preston, Esq., John Penruddock.	Wm. Ld. Howard and Elizabeth his wife.	Hynderskelfe Castle, Manors of Hovingham, Flaxton, Amotherby, Thorpe Bassett, Slyngesby, etc., etc.

YORKSHIRE FINES—*continued*

..	PLAINTIFF.	DEFORCIANT.	NATURE AND SITUATION OF PROPERTY.
1594. Easter Term, 36 Elizabeth.	Charles Cavendish, Kt.	John Atherton, Esq.	Manors of Slyngesby, Fryton, Hovingham, and 100 messuages and 100 cottages with lands there, and in Colton and Holthorpe, also advowsons of Slyngesby, Fryton, and Hovingham Churches.
1601. Trinity Term, 43 Elizabeth.	Charles Cavendish, Kt.	Anthony Wood, Gent., and Isabella his wife.	Messuage and 4 cottages in Slingsby.

APPENDIX D

ROGER DODSWORTH'S NOTES ON SLINGSBY

Roger Dodsworth, the indefatigable collector and antiquary, was born at Newton Grange, Oswaldkirk, on April 24, 1585, dying in the seventieth year of his age, 1654. Nothing of his was published in his lifetime, but he left behind him an immense mass of information, comprised in the 162 volumes folio of MSS. lodged in the Bodleian, Oxford. Some of this work was afterwards incorporated into Dugdale's famous "Monasticon Aglicanum," but a great deal still remains unprinted and in the author's own hand-writing. Like the bee that gathers honey from every flower, Dodsworth got his stores from far and near. He studied in the Marygate Tower in York, still standing in the angle formed by the main street of Bootham and Marygate, then used as a record office and containing the books and charters taken from the monasteries at their suppression. He made transcripts of many of the muniments therein de-posited, which but for this would have been utterly lost, for at the siege of York in 1642, this tower was made the chief point of attack, and all its valu-able relics destroyed. Dodsworth had the good fortune to secure the patronage of General Fairfax, who, unlike other members of his party, was particu-larly anxious to preserve all that related to literature and art, and recognising the great value of Dods-worth's work, allowed him an annuity of £40, which was to him what the pension of Raisley Calvert was to Wordsworth, helping him to pursue his literary labours without the cares of living. Dodsworth visited nearly all the churches in Yorkshire, and took notes of what he saw, particularly the inscrip-tions. Hearne, in a transport of antiquarian zeal, blesses God that "He was pleased out of His infinite goodness to raise up so pious and dili-gent a person." The following is from the MS. notes of Dodsworth's visit to Slingsby in the Bodleian.

" MS. Dodsworth, 160, fol. 209.

" Slingsby Church, 1 July, 1619.

" Honor et amor.
Pray for the saull of Sir John Fons
person of this Church aud Chapleyne to
th'erle of Northumberland the iiij——,

Anno. 1508.

Virtus Justitia.

"Ther is in the quier a monument cross legged of one of the Wyvills, att his feet a Talbott couchinge, no inscription, a shield on his arme with 3 /XX\ and a cheif depicted, the coulors hard to see. Ther is in the east end of the toune an old house of stone called Wyvill hall. The tradition is that betwixt Malton and this toune there was sometimes a serpent that lyved upon pray of passengers, which this Wyvill and dogg did kill, when he received his deathes wound. Ther is a great hole half a mile from the toune, round within and 3 yerdes broad and more, wher this serpent lay in which tyme the street was turned a myle on the south side, which doth still show it self if any take paynes to search it Ther is in the west window per pale Ar. on \ g. 3 escallopes with quarterly or and G, in the first quarter a raven proper.

"On the steeple engraven in stone a maunch and over the castle gates, which castle, manor, and parke was the ancient possession of the Hastinges, erles of Huntingdon, now sold to Sir Charles Cavendish. Ther hath beene a church in the Castle. Slyngsby paies 8/8 a yere to the manor of T— Mowbray fee.

" Slyngsby is watered with a sweete rivulet called
Wath Beek : which hath springes upp att Gawtho—
comethe by Argholme, wher it receiveth many small
springes and comethe to Wath, which giveth it name,
thence to Fritton and by Slyngsby into Holbeck.
The mannor of Hovingham was not long since the lord
Barkleys. Wathe inter ffryton et Hovingham was a
religious house of women, now the possession of
Sir Thomas Mettham. Ther is the walls of a fine
chappell nere as bigg as the church within the
castle walls, wher they had service in tyme of warres
within themselves. Ther have beene 6 Knights of
the Wivilles that have succeeded on another att
Wyvill hall above-said and the heire of Wyvill hath
itt att this day. But not of so great estait as his
ancestors were, for one of them taking parte with
Stafford (that came to Scarboro' and tooke the
Castle) lost all his land, but only Wyvill hall which
was then in Joynture.

"Note.—Sir Marmaduke Wyvill of Constableburton Baronett
did descend from thes more antient Wyvills."

APPENDIX E

PEDIGREE OF THE MOWBRAYS, OVER-LORDS OF SLINGSBY

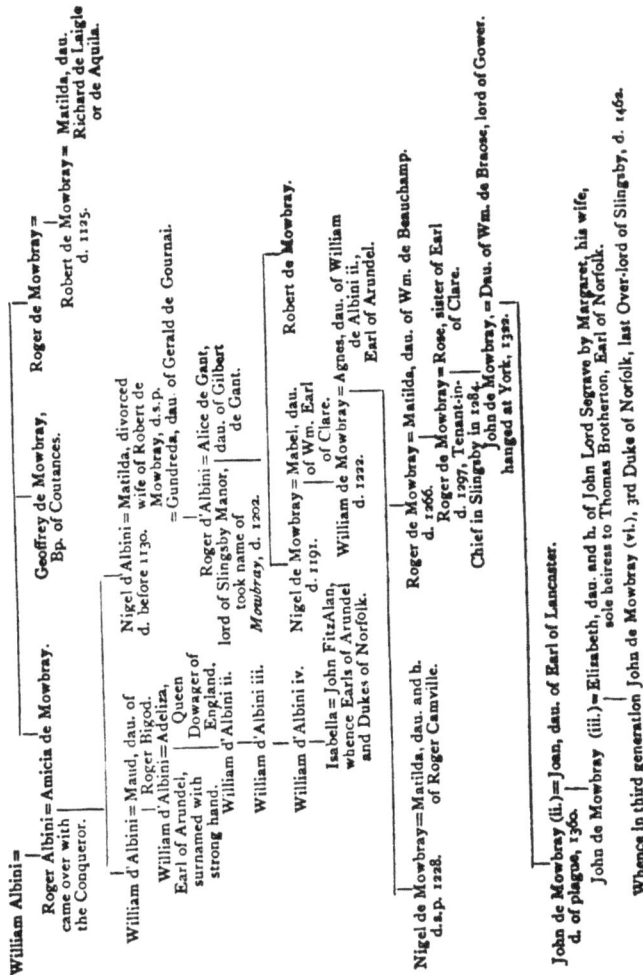

William Albini =

Roger Albini = Amicia de Mowbray. came over with the Conqueror.

Geoffrey de Mowbray, Bp. of Coutances.

Roger de Mowbray =

Robert de Mowbray = Matilda, dau. d. 1125. Richard de Laigle or de Aquila.

William d'Albini = Maud, dau. of | Roger Bigod. William d'Albini = Adeliza, Earl of Arundel, | Queen surnamed with | Dowager of strong hand. | England. William d'Albini iii.

William d'Albini iv.

Isabella = John FitzAlan, whence Earls of Arundel and Dukes of Norfolk.

Nigel d'Albini = Matilda, divorced d. before 1130. wife of Robert de Mowbray, d.s.p. = Gundreda, dau. of Gerald de Gournai.

Roger d'Albini = Alice de Gant, lord of Slingsby Manor, | dau. of Gilbert took name of | de Gant. Mowbray, d. 1202.

Nigel de Mowbray = Mabel, dau. d. 1191. of Wm. Earl of Clare.

William de Mowbray = Agnes, dau. of William d. 1222. de Albini ii, Earl of Arundel.

Robert de Mowbray.

Roger de Mowbray = Matilda, dau. of Wm. de Beauchamp. d. 1266.

Roger de Mowbray = Rose, sister of Earl d. 1297, Tenant-in- of Clare. Chief in Slingsby in 1284, John de Mowbray, = Dau. of Wm. de Braose, lord of Gower. hanged at York, 1322.

Nigel de Mowbray = Matilda, dau. and h. d.s.p. 1228. of Roger Camville.

John de Mowbray (ii.) = Joan, dau. of Earl of Lancaster. d. of plague, 1360.

John de Mowbray (iii.) = Elizabeth, dau. and h. of John Lord Segrave by Margaret, his wife, sole heiress to Thomas Brotherton, Earl of Norfolk.

Whence in third generation John de Mowbray (vi.), 3rd Duke of Norfolk, last Over-lord of Slingsby, d. 1462.

APPENDIX F

PEDIGREE OF THE HASTINGS OF SLINGSBY

Robert de Hastings, portgrave of Hastings, temp. William I., whence descended in the 10th generation

Sir Ralph de Hastings = Margaret, dau. of Sir Wm. de Herle. licensed to crenolate in Slingsby 1344. died 1346.

Isabel, dau. Sir Robert de = Sir Ralph Hastings = Maud, dau. of Sir Robert adyngton—1st wife. died 1398, seized as de Sutton of Sutton in of fee of Slingsby Holderness—2nd wife. Castle and Manor.

Margaret, only child, married 1st Sir Roger Heron—2nd Sir John Blacket.

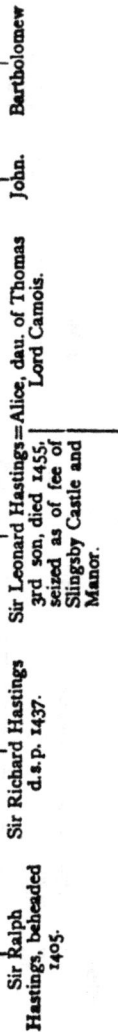

Sir Richard Hastings d.s.p. 1437.

Sir Leonard Hastings = Alice, dau. of Thomas 3rd son, died 1455, Lord Camois. seized as of fee of Slingsby Castle and Manor.

John.   Bartholomew.

Sir Ralph Hastings, beheaded 1405.

APPENDIX F—continued

PEDIGREE OF THE HASTINGS OF SLINGSBY—continued

William Hastings, = Catherine, dau. of Richard
1st Baron Hastings   Neville, Earl of Salisbury.
licensed to creno-
late in Slingsby
1462. died 1483.

    3 other sons   3 daughters.

Sir Edward Hastings, = Mary, dau. of Thomas
2nd Baron Hastings,   Baron Hungerford.
lord of Slingsby
Manor, died 1507.

Sir George Hastings, = Anne, dau. of Henry
1st Earl of Hunt-   Stafford, 2nd Duke
ingdon, died 1544.   of Buckingham.

Sir Francis Hastings, = Katherine, dau. of Henry Pole,
2nd Earl of Hun-   Lord Montacute.
tingdon, died 1560.
Parted with Slingsby
to John Yorke, 1549.

Henry Hastings, 3rd Earl = Catherine, dau. of John
of Huntingdon. Parted   Dudley Duke of Nor-
with Slingsby Manor to   thumberland.
John Atherton in 1563,
died 1595, s.p.

George Hastings, = Dorothy, dau. of
4th Earl of   Sir John Port of
Huntingdon,   Etwall.
died 1607.

    4 sons.   5 daughters.

APPENDIX G

PEDIGREE OF THE CAVENDISHES OF SLINGSBY

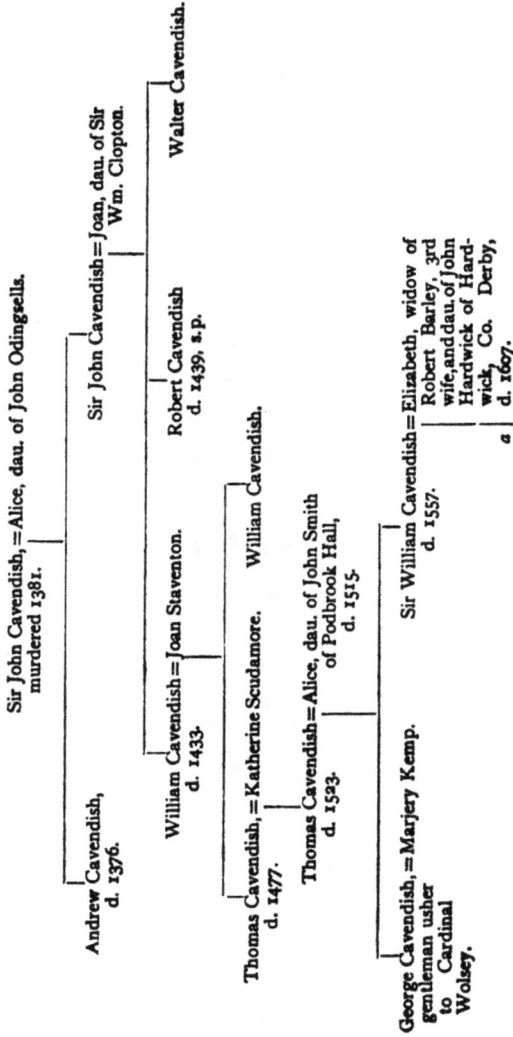

Sir John Cavendish, = Alice, dau. of John Odingsells. murdered 1381.

Andrew Cavendish, d. 1376.

Sir John Cavendish = Joan, dau. of Sir Wm. Clopton.

William Cavendish = Joan Staventon. d. 1433.

William Cavendish.

Robert Cavendish d. 1439, s.p.

Walter Cavendish.

Thomas Cavendish, = Katherine Scudamore. d. 1477.

Thomas Cavendish = Alice, dau. of John Smith of Podbrook Hall, d. 1515.

George Cavendish, = Marjery Kemp. gentleman usher to Cardinal Wolsey.

Sir William Cavendish = Elizabeth, widow of Robert Barley, 3rd wife, and dau. of John Hardwick of Hardwick, Co. Derby, d. 1557. d. 1607.

a

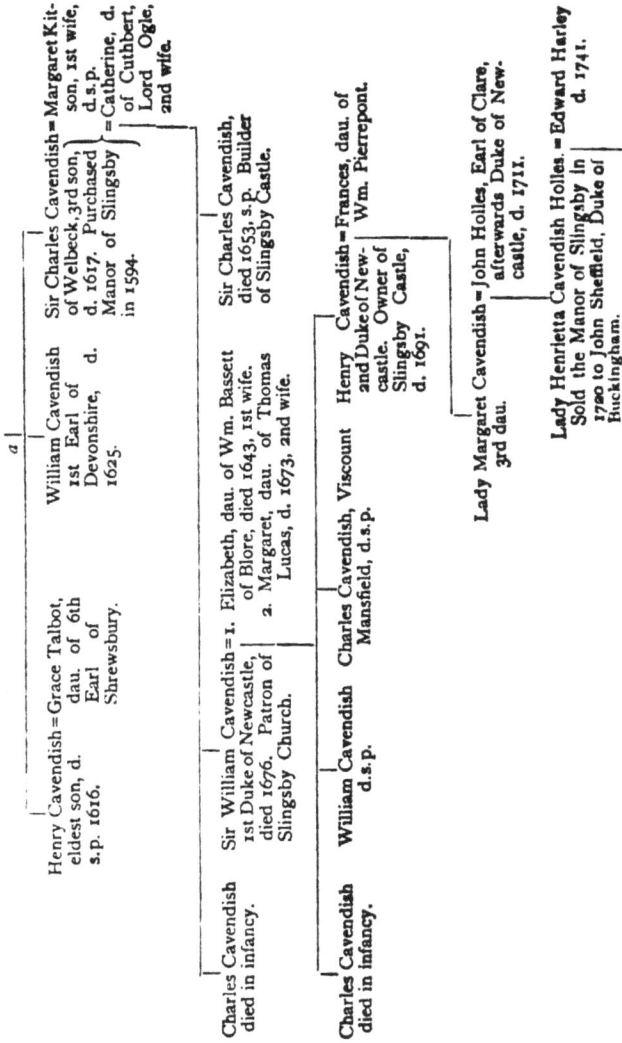

APPENDIX G—*continued*

PEDIGREE OF THE CAVENDISHES OF SLINGSBY—*continued*

a

Henry Cavendish = Grace Talbot, eldest son, d. dau. of 6th s.p. 1616. Earl of Shrewsbury.

William Cavendish 1st Earl of Devonshire, d. 1625.

Sir Charles Cavendish = Margaret Kitson, 1st wife, of Welbeck, 3rd son, d.s.p. d. 1617. Purchased Manor of Slingsby in 1594. = Catherine, d. of Cuthbert, Lord Ogle, 2nd wife.

Sir Charles Cavendish, died 1653, s.p. Builder of Slingsby Castle.

Charles Cavendish died in infancy.

Sir William Cavendish = 1. Elizabeth, dau. of Wm. Bassett 1st Duke of Newcastle, of Blore, died 1643, 1st wife. died 1676. Patron of 2. Margaret, dau. of Thomas Slingsby Church. Lucas, d. 1673, 2nd wife.

Charles Cavendish, Viscount Mansfield, d.s.p.

Henry Cavendish = Frances, dau. of and Duke of New- Wm. Pierrepont. castle. Owner of Slingsby Castle, d. 1691.

William Cavendish d.s.p.

Charles Cavendish died in infancy.

Lady Margaret Cavendish = John Holles, Earl of Clare, 3rd dau. afterwards Duke of New- castle, d. 1711.

Lady Henrietta Cavendish Holles = Edward Harley Sold the Manor of Slingsby in d. 1741. 1720 to John Sheffield, Duke of Buckingham.

APPENDIX H

ROUGH LIST OF SLINGSBY BIRDS, CONTRIBUTED BY
MR JAMES BRIGHAM OF SLINGSBY

Rapacious Birds.—A Peregrine Falcon, though not a woodland bird, was shot in the wood; only the smaller species are left, protected by their small size. The Kestrel and Sparrow-Hawk are common; and the Merlin visits us in the autumn on its way from the breeding ground on the moors to its winter quarters on the mud flats and estuaries of the South.

Owls.—We have the Barn Owl, the Long-eared Owl, the Short-eared Owl, a migrant sometimes found in turnip fields in autumn, and the Tawny or Wood Owl, although I seldom hear its well-known hoot, and am afraid it has become scarce. The Great Grey Shrike has been shot here. The Pied Flycatcher once obtained here; the Spotted Flycatcher common. The Swallow, Martin, Sand-Martin, Swift, very numerous. The Titmice common: the Great Titmouse and Blue Titmouse in the village, and the Coal-Marsh and Long-tailed species in the wood; the White Wagtail, Pied Wagtail common, and the Yellow Wagtail; the Wren common, the Creeper, and Nuthatch in the wood; the Common Bunting, Yellow-Hammer Bunting very numerous, and Reed Bunting.

Of the *Crow Family*, the Carrion Crow, the Hooded Crow, Rook, and Jackdaw are common. The Magpie sometimes breeds with us, but is often driven off. The Jay still exists in the wood in spite of the keeper; the Raven, a vanishing Yorkshire, and I may say British, bird, bred on the mausoleum at Castle Howard up to about 1850. I saw the old birds and the nest a few years before that date, and it might be then said to be a Slingsby bird, as the nesting-place was within two miles of our parish boundary.

Thrushes.—We have the Missel-Thrush, Song Thrush or Throstle Blackbird; Ring Ouzel once killed on its migration to the moors where it breeds; Fieldfare, Redwing, and Dipper which comes to our beck in winter, but does not stay to breed. Wheat-ear, Whinchat, Redstart, Redbreast, White-throat, Lesser White-throat, Blackcap rare. Garden-Warbler rare. Gold-crested Wren and Chiff-chaff in the wood. Willow-Wren very numerous; Wood-Wren rare; Sedge-Warbler common; Grasshopper Warbler a very rare summer visitant. I heard this bird at the same place for two seasons, but from its skulking habits could not see it. Hedge Sparrow common; Meadow Pipit or Titlark; Tree Pipit, a spring migrant breeding near the railway. The Skylark is an interesting bird from the fact, which appears to be clearly ascertained, that the home-bred birds migrate southward in the autumn, and that the large flocks we have in winter are immigrants from the North.

Of the *Fringilla* family we have some beautiful species: the Goldfinch still breeds in the village, and we have the Chaffinch; the Greenfinch, the

Mountain-finch or Brambling sometimes comes in
very hard winters; the Linnet, the Lesser Redpole,
the Bullfinch breed in the wood, and in winter a few
come into the lanes; the Hawfinch is a new bird
here, and has come to breed, and be a resident in the
village within the last ten years; this fine bird is so
shy that it would rarely be seen but for its unfortunate
habit of destroying garden peas after the young
birds leave the nest; the Starling very numerous.
I once noticed a light-coloured bird in a large
flock which I thought was a Rose-coloured
Starling or Pastor, which is a rare casual visitant;
the House Sparrow very numerous; Tree Sparrow
not uncommon, but from its shy habits it is not often
distinguished from the common species; the Cuckoo
common, the Pied Wagtail being the usual foster
parent here; Woodpeckers, the Greater Spotted and
the Green, are common, the Lesser Spotted very
rare; the Kingfisher may often be seen at the beck,
where its favourite breeding-place has been destroyed
by rabbits; the Crossbill, a very rare winter visitor;
the Nightjar sometimes seen but not common; the
Heron may often be seen on the beck; the Peewit
common; Ring Dotterel, one shot at the Carr;
Woodcock, winter visitor, once found breeding in
the wood; Snipe common at the Carr, where it bred
for several years; the Sandpiper breed on the streams
near the Carr; Redshank, one of a pair of breeding
birds shot at the Carr; Greenshank very rare, one
shot at the Carr; Little Stint very rare, one shot at
the Carr; Water Rail, not common, has been found

at the Carr; Land Rail common; Water Hen common; Jack Snipe rare; Curlew uncommon here, but
three birds, probably young, were seen about the
sheep-walk for some weeks in the autumn; Golden
Plover at the Carr in autumn often in large flocks;
Coot; Avocet—I have a memorandum that I saw
two Avocets at Slingsby beck, near the Carr, on
7th September 1871. This bird is now extinct as a
British breeding bird; the Bittern no doubt bred in
the Carr before the embankment was made to keep
out flood water. An old friend of mine, bred and
born close to the place more than one hundred years
ago, used often to tell me that an old man informed
him and others how the Butter-bump used to boom
from the middle of a hay-bock in the Carr. Of
course the hay-cock was a mistake, the boom would
come from the reeds and rushes in the swampy parts.
The American Bittern, a bird of extremely rare
occurrence in this country, was shot at Kells Springs,
4th December 1871, and seen by me in the flesh;
it was set up by Graham, the York taxidermist,
and sold by him for the collection of Sir John Crewe.
A flock of Wild Swans or Whooper seen and heard;
Wild Geese—a Bernicle shot at the Carr, 29th
December 1876; Pink-footed Goose, the common
wild goose of the country, may be seen in October
flying in straight line or in the form of a wedge
over this township from the stubble-fields on the
high wolds to Scotland, always flying in the same
direction, north by west. Possibly some of the other
grey geese may come the same way, such as the

Grey Lag, Bean Goose, and White-fronted Goose, but these are rare in Yorkshire.

Ducks.—We have the Mallard, Wigeon, Teal, Shoveller, and the Pintail and Common Scoter, which are sea ducks, have been shot at the Carr; other species frequent the lake at Castle Howard, such as the Pochard, Tufted Duck, and Golden-eye, and probably sometimes frequent the Carr. I cannot claim that fine bird the Goosander, although it always frequents the lake in winter, but the Great Northern Diver was shot at the Carr, and the Sclavonian Grebe and Little Grebe or Dabchick have been obtained here.

Pigeons.—The Ring Dove or Wood Pigeon numerous. Stock Dove began to breed in the old castle about thirty years ago, and was unknown here forty years since. Turtle Dove once seen. Pallas's Sand Grouse observed on the wing in the summer of 1888.

Game Birds.—Pheasants and Partridges numerous in favourable breeding seasons.

INDEX

TURNBULL AND SPEARS, PRINTERS, EDINBURGH